FAT BLACK GIRL IN A WHEELCHAIR #3

"DOOR # 3"

TABLE OF CONTENTS

So I'm wondering...

How are Biden and Harris going to herd all these cats should they win? At this point they have almost everyone's endorsement except the most hardcore members of Sir Bluster's death cult. That's one crowded, crazy ass tent, no matter how big you'd like it to be. Once you pull the country back from the brink of disaster, what have you really got? What's really behind Door #3?

REASONS FOR BEING BORN...

Well: here I am, almost a year after my last issue. A little older, a little more confused. Everything and nothing has changed. History doesn't exactly repeat, but it rhymes, and it rhymes hard.

Last month the Sir Bluster Reality Circus officially ended. We now have a nice, normal President who speaks in complete sentences and doesn't make up his own alternative facts. Plus he's from my home state -- Delaware -- so that's a bonus. However, Sir Bluster's fandom didn't want the show to end, so on January 6th, they stormed the Capitol hoping to stop the steal. It was literally a hell of a finale.

But even though Sir Bluster's reign of terror in the White House is over, we're hardly out of the woods. While he was preoccupied with the care and feeding of his boundless ego, a pandemic ravaged the country and we lost over half a Delaware's worth of people, and the real economy, as opposed to the stock market, tanked. Despite the fact we now have potentially three vaccines to help mitigate the spread of COVID-19, we still aren't home free. While other countries already had some respect for the commons, robust social safety nets, and a national health care infrastructure, we're having to make stuff up on the fly. President Biden and his team are trying their damndest, but it may be too little, too late. Things will get worse before they get better. While Biden's victory may have saved us from an immediate Robert Mugabe Zimbabwe style collapse, the road ahead is uphill both ways and littered with potholes. It's hard to win a race when you have to dig yourself out of a hole just to reach the starting line. Sir Bluster's damage will linger like a bad smell for years to come.

The sad thing is, if it weren't for the virus putting the fear of death in a critical mass of people, I believe Sir Bluster might have won a second term. And *that* would have been the end of the country as we know it. As an old co-worker used to say, "the fear that somebody brown might get something" runs deep.

The folks who participated in the January 6th Insurrection weren't the desperate poor. They were business owners, off duty cops, sons of judges, respectable people who lived in an alternative universe.

The really odd thing about the Capitol Riot was that two months earlier, I began writing a novel which takes place in a reconstituted United States (now called the New Union) after a Second Civil War. The novel began as a diversion to keep me from obsessing about election results.

When I first began submitting chapters to my writing group, everyone thought I was being terribly morose. Surely, I didn't expect violence after a Biden victory. *I don't know, I wrote in an email. I hope it doesn't come to that, but 45 and*

On the afternoon of January 6th, I received an email: *Crap.
You definitely called that one.*

The Animal House Rebellion wasn't exactly a Fort Sumpter
moment, but without accountability, it will become a dress
rehearsal for one.

The virus and our nation's hungry ghosts aren't the only
things that ail us. The earth is fairly pissed too. We had
record wildfire and hurricane seasons and our husk of a
government couldn't adequately deal with any of it. That's
what 40 years of starving the beast gets you.

***

I am still pretty much housebound. It's been a year since I've
actually been inside a grocery store to buy groceries, eaten
in a restaurant, or been inside a library. I have bought
precisely seven tanks of gas in the last eleven months. I
used to get out fairly regularly to see the doctor, but now,
that's mostly online. I take a short drive weekly, just to make
sure the car still works and run errands, but that's about it. In
some ways my life has shrunk to the bare essentials.

But it's also expanded. I've attended more concerts,
lectures, and readings in the past year than I have in the last
ten. Fortunately, I'm one of those people who doesn't get

persnickety about seeing movies on the big screen or
seeing theater live. For one thing, I don't have to worry
about stairs or getting there early enough to snag one of the
few handicapped parking spots. And a virtual performance
is cheaper -- far cheaper. I still can't afford to see everything,
but I can scrape together $20 to see Laurie Anderson since
in a normal year it would cost at least $100. (If we ever make
it back to some semblance of "normal", I hope whatever
surviving arts venues never stop doing the virtual stuff at
affordable prices.)

***

Lockdown has been like an extended forced meditation
retreat. With all that quiet, you can't help but start thinking,
and as the months of isolation wear on, the thinking goes
deep. Sometimes I find myself hankering to hear music I
haven't thought about in ages. This summer, when riots
broke out in Wilmington, and old high school classmates
posted on social media about needing to get to the gun
shop for extra ammunition to defend the homestead in case
the mayhem spread to Hockessin (I mean, you have to see
Hockessin to realize just how ridiculous this White folk panic
was) I awoke with earworms from the early 80's. (This is
when an Apple Music subscription is a good thing.) I also
dreamed a lot about high school. Actually, I dreamed a lot in
general. Many a morning I woke up thinking, *Now what the
hell was that about?*

***

For the first time in my life, I've established a semi-regular
writing schedule. From 10 to 4, for six days a week, I work

on something. For now, it's mainly been my post Second Civil War novel, but I've also been digging out some old stuff I started just before my health problems got unbearable, one being a group of prequel stories to my book *Love in the Time of Unraveling.*

It's strange to revisit the world of the Crescent after nearly five years. When I first wrote it, it felt like the future future, like the very end of this century. Now I swear some of it might happen next week. Designer hazard wear is coming, y'all. I know it.

On with the show...

FEB. 6, 2021

Last night I watched a video of Alexandria Ocasio-Cortez talking about what happened to her on January 6th, during the raid on the Capitol, which will have its 1 month anniversary this coming Saturday. The rioters were actively looking for her and she rightfully feared for her life.

Many of the comments were disconcerting, to say the least, if not downright reprehensible. No way was she making stuff up or exaggerating her tale for effect. It makes perfect sense the rioters would be actively searching for her. Other than Nancy Pelosi, she is one of the most visible members of Congress, and a frequent recipient of Sir Bluster's derision during his disastrous reign. For better or worse, she has come to symbolize the mythical radical left, and there is no telling what that mob might've done if they'd found her. She had every reason to be terrified.

Why is she *still* talking about it a month later? I mean, shouldn't she be over it by now?

If you're asking those kinds of questions, there's at least two things you don't understand. One: the January 6th Animal House Rebellion, despite its ridiculous premise, was deadly serious business. I know there's the temptation to write it off as a glitch in the matrix just because it looked like a frat party out of control or the folks scaling the Capitol walls resembled something out of *World War Z*. But evil doesn't have to be suave, sexy, or as precisely choreographed as *Triumph of the Will* to do its damage; all it has to be is itself.

And evil is what the Capitol insurrection was. It was the near total collapse of everything this country claims to hold dear. And it *was* a bone chilling thing to watch. There's shaky cellphone video of Delaware's lone Congressperson, crouched on the floor praying like she is in church and her soul is on fire. So yeah: AOC wasn't the only one fearing for her life that day.

You also probably have little idea of how trauma works. The first thing that happens when you're in a situation where you actually fear for your life is that the ancient animal part of your brain kicks in -- y'know, the part that saved our species from saber tooth tigers and such. That part of your brain has very little language, if any. The most it will do is bark commands: *Run! Play dead! Don't cry! Scream!* If you're lucky, you might retain enough presence of mind to get a license plate number, or remember your attacker's tattoo, but that didn't work for me.

If your higher consciousness hasn't totally shut down, it's completely detached from your body, floating somewhere just below the ceiling, and making inane comments, like: *Gees, that gun looks nothing like the ones I see on TV.* Or: *Gees, gunfire sounds a lot like fireworks.*

If the situation drags on long enough, you start making bargains with a higher power, even if you don't exactly believe in one. (It's true: there are no atheists in foxholes, or hold-ups, or sexual assaults, etc.) *Please don't let me die on the floor of a fast food restaurant. Please let me live through this.* You might even get to the point where you're compelled to make peace with your imminent death. "Yep," you might say to yourself, "this is it." Or as AOC said: "If this is your plan for me, so be it. There are others to continue the work."

The really strange thing is (at least this is how it worked for me) you are never at your most fearful when the trauma is in progress. You're fearful enough to mount some sort of defense, but not so fearful that you're completely non-functional. This, I believe, is by design. The body knows what it's doing. Because if you completely collapsed, death would be certain, and your body will do anything to survive. The paralyzing fear, the anxiety attacks, the endless sleepless nights...that comes later, sometimes years later, when it suddenly hits you: *Damn, I could have died!*

So it doesn't surprise me that AOC is still talking about this. She's not faking or grandstanding. She's still processing what must have been a truly terrifying experience. Also: she wants you to know that January 6th was not merely the day the Sir Bluster Reality Circus completely jumped the shark; it was serious business and there must be accountability.

DREAMS OF LOCKDOWN

I dreamed I woke up one morning and the house was full of birds. Surprisingly, I wasn't frightened, just confused. Although I was rather annoyed when one of them flew off with my glasses. "Damn," I thought, "I'll have to replace them -- again. That's the third pair this year."

***

I dreamed they implanted an empathy chip in Sir Bluster's brain so he might catch a clue. Its first test was during a live statement he made about the passing of Ruth Bader Ginsburg.

The only reason we watched the speech at all was to see if and how the chip worked.

It didn't. While there was no sniffling, mispronunciations, and run-on sentences, and the tone of his voice sounded genuinely mournful, nothing he said made any sense. "I know this news is difficult, but look outside: your lawn is green." "I cannot promise you justice tonight, but I can offer you toy food."

"Toy food," Mom repeated laughing. "Yep, that's what he gives us. That's the first time he's told the truth."

***

I dreamed that a group of us met at Skyline Middle School to receive our papers to leave the country. As I pulled into the parking lot, I noticed some folks in the crowd I knew, mixed with strangers.

The whole thing was a lottery type operation. You were invited by the resistance to submit an application of intent and they would match you with a new country. You wouldn't know where you were going until you were handed your new passport. All I had was the clothes on my back, a duffle bag of my belongings, about €2000 (that was the most valuable currency) my cane, and a secondhand wheelchair.

For those of you non locals, Skyline Middle School sits near the second highest point in Delaware. If you stand on the sidewalk, and look out over the basketball courts, on a clear day you can see the Delaware Memorial Bridge and into the state of New Jersey.

Anyway: on that morning, I stood on the sidewalk and saw three statues flying over the bridge attached to wires. The first was the head of the Statue of Liberty, the second was a bald eagle, that in the dream world at least, was from the top of the Federal Reserve building. The third statue head kept changing: it was Susan B. Anthony, John Lewis, Bobby Kennedy, Allen Ginsburg, Harriet Tubman, Frederick Douglas, Cole Porter... and that's all I can remember. I thought: "There they go. All the American Saints."

The really weird thing is this strange sight did not have the otherworldly quality of a vision. I got the feeling all these heads were actually being carted someplace. Then all three heads dropped from the sky and the bridge collapsed, leaving a blood red cloud in its place.

I got inside the school as fast as I could. "It's Year Null!" I cried. "Those fools are trying to erase history!"

That's when I was handed my new passport. I was going to Cuba.

"But I barely know any Spanish," I protested.

"But you are an artist. You can do your good from there."

***

I dreamed I was a court reporter in a court which tried juveniles who committed heinous crimes. The young lady on trial that particular day was accused of animal genocide.

There was a certain lake where on the Winter Solstice the rare pearl backed turtle would gather. Pearl backed turtles were prized for their pearly white rainbow iridescent shells. On the night of the gathering, if the moon was out, and the sky was clear, it looked as if the lake was dotted with glowing stones. The young lady on trial had traveled to the lake on the night of this magical gathering and somehow set every last turtle at the lake on fire. This single act drove the species to the brink of extinction.

The judge asked the accused: "What caused you to do this awful thing?"

The girl answered: "My mother instructed me to call the spirit of Loki Adonis, the spirit of greed, chaos, and suffering, so that we might reap what we have sown."

"Well," said the judge, handing down her sentence, "now you must return to the lake, light a candle for every life lost, and weep sincerely without ceasing for the rest of your days."

The girl's mother immediately objected. "But Your Honor, that isn't fair! Would you cause me to lose my child forever? Her life has just begun!"

The judge was unmoved. "Surely every soul in that lake had a dream as luminous as your daughter's and your own. Was it fair to deny those dreams? My sentence stands."

***

I dreamed I was interviewing people at a pyromaniac's convention. I was sitting in the lounge of a fancy hotel talking to this one man about why he loved fire. "Fire," he explained, "is the most beautiful state of matter on earth. It's sensual, dangerous, and mystical all at once. I love the smell, the sound...everything. There is no greater thrill than a good burn."

"What do you do at a pyro convention?"

He shrugged. "Lots of stuff. Trade info on the best accelerants, talk about our best burns, watch film..."

"Films? Pyro porn?"

He laughed. "I never thought of it that way, but I guess it is."

I asked him what he did when he wasn't at the convention.

"Burn ruins, mostly...and trash. I light the flames and am transported."

"Is it legal?" I asked.

He winked. "Mostly. But it's always lucrative."

He invited me to the convention highlight -- a collective burn in a fallow field about 10 miles from the hotel. "It's basically a huge bonfire, showcasing our best work," he explained. "I hear tell someone has mastered the elusive rainbow flame, the pyro's dream. I once made one by accident, but this guy can summon one consistently. You won't believe the visions you can see in one of those. You can transcend time and space."

I was tempted, but in the end, I declined. "Thanks, but no thanks," I said.

N*GGA LESSONS

The first time I remember being called the n-word was on the first day of first grade. All the kids were lined up in alphabetical order on the blacktop, separated by teacher and grade. A boy in the line next to mine shouted it at me. To tell you the truth, I wasn't sure what it meant, but I could tell from his tone of voice it wasn't something good.

First, I checked my shoes. Were they on the correct foot? I knew I had trouble telling left from right, probably because I hadn't decided which hand was better to write with (I figured you had two hands, so one could relieve the other) but as far as I could tell and feel, I'd managed not to screw things up that morning. I knew my clothes were clean and pressed. Mom wouldn't have let me out of the house otherwise. I felt my head. As far as I could feel, all hairs were still shellacked in place.

I figured the boy just sensed I was strange, and I was, but my cootie situation must've been critical for some random boy in a new school to pick up on it so quickly.

I didn't cry. I was just confused. Then: my teacher came out to lead our class into the building, and it was over for that day. Later, after dinner, when I asked my parents about it, they would explain the n-word was a bad word for Negro, and to be prepared, because a lot of White kids might call me that.

Why? I asked.

Nastiness, they replied. *But you can't be nasty back.*

***

My parents grew up in the Jim Crow south, but they didn't lecture me about race unless it was absolutely necessary. When I was older, they would explain this was because they didn't want me to have a chip on my shoulder. If you go out into the world expecting a fight, it's more likely to come to you.

Now, don't get me wrong; I knew I was different. I could plainly see my skin was darker; my hair was kinky and dry, and grew up and out, instead of straight down, like my classmates, or the hippie girls I saw on TV. I could hear my parents listened to different music -- the Supremes, Marvin Gaye, Stevie Wonder, Jr. Walker and the All Stars -- instead of the Beatles and Rolling Stones.

I knew there were an unwritten set of rules I had to follow because of the color of my skin. I never could go out in public looking frumpy. I had to make sure I had impeccable manners. *Sir, Ma'am, Mr., Mrs., Please, Thank you*, without exception. I had to work extra hard to get perfect grades. I didn't get to coast like my White classmates, because if I screwed up, even a little, I made things more difficult not just for me, but for all little dark girls like me. I was an ambassador for my people whether I liked it or not.

Though I didn't have the easiest childhood, I didn't immediately chalk it up to being a Black girl in a mostly White world. I knew I was a bonefide weirdo. I could read before I entered the first grade -- I'd been doing it since I was three -- but I didn't read well aloud because I had horrible stage fright. I stuttered, stammered, and mispronounced even familiar words. This caused teachers to assume I read poorly, and would often lead to me getting tracked lower until my mother went to the school and made a fuss. (Which, of course, only made matters worse. No one wants to be the kid whose mother is always at the school.)

What confused my teachers even more, was that I wrote far better than I talked. (Looking back, this makes sense because that's the way I first acquired language. I wrote in complete sentences before I spoke in them.) My written expression was so far ahead of my oral expression that I was often accused of cheating when I turned in my notebooks.

I was also a fat klutz, which made gym class torture. (On top of that, I hit puberty early, which made the required communal showers a nightmare.) Besides: I didn't like to play like other kids. I liked to read, to write "radio" plays for the intercom system in the house, as well as songs and stories. I was fascinated with current events, even those beyond my understanding.

So: there were plenty of reasons I wasn't Ms. Popular — and most of them had nothing to do with being Black.

The only time my parents spoke freely about their experiences with American apartheid was when we made the annual road trip down South to visit my extended family. Usually these tales were spun late at night, when the coals in the grill had burned to ash, the games of badminton and Twister were over, and the grownups had a few beers in them. That's when you would learn about the forgotten intricacies of segregated water fountain etiquette, hear about the Black dentist who got sentenced to nine months on a chain gang for not relinquishing a party line for a White woman, or one of my older cousins would tell the story about when she had a hankering for ice cream and her father stopped at a general store in rural Georgia, and he was told to go to the colored entrance around back. These tales sounded positively surreal and spooky, like the ghost stories I heard around the campfire at Girl Scout camp. It was difficult to believe they actually happened. It was astounding folks could ever be that cruel and stupid.

We learned about the Civil War and slavery in school, but when you're a kid, all events before your birth seem equally unreal and distant. You know the Civil War happened way after Moses and the dinosaurs, but it was still ancient history. Humans were better now; they had to be. (Well, except for World War 2 and the Holocaust, but that could be blamed on mass hysteria like the Salem Witch Trials. A temporary glitch in the system.)

You learned slavery was bad in a nebulous sense, but you were never taught all the violence it entailed. There was no mention of rape, or branding, or coffles. There was the forced labor, but without the messy blood and death. You learned the Civil War was fought over "economics" and "state's rights". You were taught that while there were a few exceptionally evil slave owners who reveled in the master's role (think Simon Legree from *Uncle Tom's Cabin*) most were otherwise good, upstanding people who didn't know any better. Those exceptionally evil masters had their analogues in the present -- those were the bad apples the good Reverend King fought so hard against, the ones that wore hoods, burned crosses, and bombed churches -- but most present day Whites were bewildered innocents, trapped in a self-perpetuating juggernaut over which they had no control.

I think I was a freshman in college before I began to understand the monumental evils of slavery and systemic racism.

But I digress... I was talking about being Black.

Race did not become onerous until I hit puberty and found myself the only Black girl in a mostly White, mostly male, mostly wealthy Catholic school. My parents decided (wisely, although it didn't feel like it at the time) that I would get lost at the public high school in my district with 2000+ students, so they started searching for alternatives. They ferried me to a series of entrance exams at modestly priced parochial and private schools in the area.

I wound up being part of the first class of girls at an exclusive Catholic high school near the Delaware-Pennsylvania border. Frankly, it was a wonder I was accepted because I took their entrance exam while having the worst cramps in my life. This was a rigorous bare bones school, with none of that art or music foolishness. (Although I hear they have some of that foolishness now) Just a straight college prep track with 3+ hours of homework a night. Graduates were accepted at Ivy League colleges and went on to be pillars of the community: doctors, lawyers, business owners, Senators. It didn't especially sound like fun, but my parents were never for this learning is fun crap. School was deadly serious business; it was a job -- not a game.

Since I lived at the wrong end of I-95, my parents had to drive me to the bus stop on Union St. in Wilmington. This meant my day started early; I had to be up by 5:00 AM on school days. From Union St., the bus took a tour through the wealthier subdivisions in town, until I finally arrived at school just before 8:00.

Academically, I held my own. I wasn't a genius, but I brought home A's and B's. English teachers told me I had a fine command of the language; math teachers said I could be an engineer one day if I only applied myself -- but since I loathed math, my heart was never in it.

Socially, I had problems from the start. I was one of two Black students in the whole school, two of out of 400. The other Black student, a boy named Lynn, had a more harrowing commute than I did. He took the commuter train down from Philadelphia. He did have an advantage over me, though; he played sports. (The school had no art and music, but it did have one of the best football teams in the state.) Well-meaning students tried to make the two of us a couple because we "matched". We both resented it.

High school was also where I found out that while my family wasn't poor, we were far from wealthy. My classmates went to mythical (well, mythical to me since I had no chance in hell of ever going there) places like the Bahamas and Europe on their summer vacations, while I always went to Arkansas and Alabama.

I did find a couple of friends among the misfits, but I'm only in contact with a few people from my high school years, only one of whom actually went to my high school.

Junior year things got bad. Despite my early puberty, it took me until 16 to have my first real crushes. I had two. One was on a girl at church who played guitar in a Christian rock band and was one of the first people who took my songwriting seriously; the other was a boy at my school, who was just as socially awkward as I was, who liked science fiction, and taught me how to play chess. We used to spend hours on the phone discussing science fiction novels and nothing in particular.

I felt there was something true between us -- well as much as any 16 year old can know these things -- and I was so sure he was going to ask me to prom. He did not. He asked a sophomore who didn't even know how to pluck her eyebrows. It came as a total shock. I'd never even seen them together in the hallways.

I maintained a brave face on the bus after I got the news. I knew enough not to make a scene in public. I tried to convince myself this rejection made some logical sense. The other girl might have shaved her eyebrows down to nothing, but she was thin and fashionable. My mother had been after me to lose weight. Maybe this rejection was my punishment for not listening. I had brought this on myself.

Still, the boy remained friendly to me as if nothing had happened. The next morning he sat next to me on the bus while I held back my tears. He started talking about some book he was reading. I said nothing.

Why are you being so quiet? he asked.

I shrugged. *No reason*, I mumbled while staring out the window.

We rode in silence for a bit. Finally, a couple of stops before we arrived at school, he made his confession. *Listen*, he whispered, *I would have asked you. But my parents don't believe in mixed dating.*

Well. There was my reason. No amount of dieting or wardrobe refresh was going to fix that.

I'm sure he told me this to make me feel better. He wanted me to know he still liked me, but you know...parents...society...the world... They all get in the way.

I didn't say anything. I managed to make it to lunchtime without my broken heart spilling over. But instead of heading to the cafeteria at lunch, I locked myself in a far stall in the girl's bathroom and cried so hard I gave myself the dry heaves. Somebody came in and heard me choking on my teenage angst, and fearing I had maybe broken a bone and really hurt myself, ran and got the school nurse, who was justifiably concerned.

She asked me several times what was wrong, but of course, I couldn't explain it. How do you explain to a White nurse how bad that hurt? I wasn't being melodramatic when I sobbed, *You wouldn't understand!* I was telling the gospel truth.

 My parents were no better than the nurse. While they certainly understood the social dynamics of the situation, they were unsympathetic. I was living in a fantasy world. Whites would only let me in so far. I shouldn't have expected the boy to ask me in the first place. So I cried some more. I cried so much, I think I literally cried myself a river that day.

Things went downhill from there. I stopped eating, stopped sleeping, stopped doing homework. I came within inches of failing out. Finally, I got some counseling and reached a sort of equilibrium. I was done with all that romance stuff. I was going to be a virgin hermit poet. Race doesn't matter if you never leave the house.

Actually, it wasn't just counseling that helped me survive this. During my junior year, the school hired a new English teacher who had an interest in drama and the school put on some plays. One of these was a musical, so an upright piano got moved into the auditorium where masses and school assemblies were held.

Though I auditioned for several plays, and was actually a fairly decent actor, I knew ahead of time I would never get any lead parts. Most of the plays we put on had a romantic couple as the leads and there was no way they were going to have an interracial couple -- even a pretend one -- on that stage. (Of course, no one but my parents ever said this to my face; they always had some other excuse. "That was a good audition, but your voices don't match," which I always took to mean my speaking voice was ugly. Or maybe: "That was a good audition, but you're not tall enough." But I wasn't short either; I was average height.) Still, I always got some kind of part, which was enough to feel like I belonged, and enough to get me into the cast party.

The piano in the auditorium did something else: it helped me to show off my songwriting, which helped make the bus rides to school much more pleasant.

By my junior year there were enough kids from my side of town to warrant the bus stopping closer to my house. One of the kids who now rode the bus was the son of a mortician, and he used to torment me mercilessly. I'm not sure why. Maybe it was because he knew he could get a rise out of me, or maybe he secretly liked me. Maybe he thought I was a weirdo. Who knows?

He was certainly weird. He used to bring his father's mortician manuals on the bus to gross people out. I never found the pictures inside gross; Instead, I was curious and always asked questions. Of course, he never knew the answer. He'd just brought the books to shock us. Anyway: he made bus rides a living hell for a few months, which is damn near forever in adolescent time. But I didn't tell any adults about it. It was kind of embarrassing to be tormented by an annoying kid two grades younger than me.

Anyway: one afternoon I was alone in the auditorium playing piano before rehearsal started. Somewhere in there he snuck in and took a seat behind me.

I didn't know you could play piano, he said when I was through. I noticed his tone of voice was respectful; for once he wasn't mocking me.

Yeah, I said. *I took lessons for several years.* Then, since I had his attention, I played him one of the songs I'd written. I can't remember which one, but it probably sounded like something off of Joni Mitchell's *Hejira,* since that album was the soundtrack to my junior year.

After I finished, he asked: *You actually wrote that?* Again, he didn't sound condescending at all. He almost sounded awestruck, like he'd just completely rewritten the biography he had imagined for me.

Yeah, I replied, somewhat embarrassed.

Can I hear something else?

I checked the time. *Sure.*

I played until the other cast members began to show up.

After that impromptu concert, the mortician's son never bothered me on the bus again. That's when I learned: art can keep your ass from getting bullied.

***

Art did something else: it helped me transform the pain into something beautiful, and by doing that, it helped me survive. I'm not exaggerating when I talk about survival. Between the fallout from awkward chess boy and Christian rock guitar girl, I didn't exactly have a banner year in the romance department. I attempted suicide that spring.

I don't think I actually wanted to die, because I don't think I quite understood what death was. I had known only one kid my age who died -- he passed away from leukemia in the 8th grade -- but he had been sick, bald, and in pain for most of that year. Although I missed him when he disappeared (because that's what it felt like, one day he simply vanished) I was somewhat relieved because it meant for him all the pain and teasing (for being bald) had finally stopped.

And that's precisely what I sought from death: I wanted the pain to stop. Forever.

The thing was: for me, that burning desire for oblivion -- those fraught moments actively staring down the abyss -- weren't constant. Someone could've talked me off the ledge if they'd found me in time and had the patience to listen long enough. But I had no one. For most of that spring, my depression manifested as overwhelming fatigue and a painful numbness -- if that makes any sense. I had plenty of feelings, but no safe place, nor the energy, to express them, so I flattened everything into a smoldering gray haze.

The biggest thing I felt after my suicide attempt was shame, and I made a pact with myself to never sink that low again. My inability to deal with rejection and reality had caused my family the needless expense and embarrassment of a family psychologist. Back when they grew up, children learned quickly the world wasn't fair, bit the bullet, and accepted it. You quickly learned there were places you didn't go, and things you couldn't do, and you became an expert at navigating the minefield. You learned to survive, and perhaps, to thrive.

So: while I could go to the White people school, have a fine command of the language, and get decent grades, it was foolish of me, to ever expect to truly belong. As someone tells the enslaved main character in Ta-Nahesi Coates' *The Water Dancer* when he is "promoted" to the main house because he is his master's bastard son: "Those people ain't your family." Watch, listen, and learn all you can in the master's house, but keep your shields up, and know when to move on.

I grudgingly erected myself a wall and engaged those shields, but I still needed a place to dump all those pesky feelings. The psychologist suggested keeping a diary, so I was a dedicated diarist for a week, until I found my daily minutia bored the crap out of me. Unfiltered, I couldn't even hold my own interest, so I mined my pain for raw material for songs, poems, and stories instead. That, at least, made my pain interesting to me -- and bonus -- it made it interesting for others too, and gave me a way to connect to the outside world.

I was a junior in high school when I first unconsciously formulated something I call The Artist's Prayer. *Oh Universe, I promise, if you let me live through this, I will turn it on its head and make it beautiful.* It remains the closest thing I have to a religion.

But art did not only allow me to transform pain into beauty; it also allowed me to speak my truth in a way that was safe for me and others. You couldn't risk speaking raw truth to power in class, because that would risk your grade, which in turn would risk your standing with adults in your life who mattered. You couldn't address the truth of your pain in your daily interactions because that only brought friction, alienation, and loneliness. *Why do you want to talk about that stuff? It's depressing. Why are you so angry? Why are you so sensitive? Why can't you be positive and be thankful for what you have?* So while I maintained a polished and polite exterior, I didn't go completely silent. If I had tried that, I probably would not be around to write this today.

I discovered art was the one place where you could scream out loud and you didn't frighten people. Even a sloppily confessional slam poem, or a slightly offensive monologue is easier for most people to take than the unvarnished truth. "I can't even tell something true unless it has a punchline behind it," Dave Chapelle jokingly lamented during his opening monologue on the *Saturday Night Live* episode just after the 2020 election. "You guys aren't ready. You're not ready for this."

My survival strategy wasn't unique. My ancestors have been doing it for ages. That's where all that Black people magic comes from -- from spirituals, to gospel, to jazz, to hip hop, to spoken word, to house music, and so on -- mining the pain into gold.

I wondered what would have become of me if my race and personal quirks had not forced me to muster the inner resources to cope. What if I had found no place to put my anguish? Would I have turned to drugs or alcohol? They were ubiquitous in high school, but for some odd reason, I was never tempted, even though I desperately ached to belong.

More recently I took powerful opiates for two years due to overwhelming chronic pain, but somehow managed to never get addicted, even though by the end of those two years, I'd lost my job due to my chronic pain and poor health and was nearly flat broke. Did doodling in Illustrator, which I did almost obsessively during that long decline, save my life, even though the version I had was years out of date? How did I not become a statistic? How come I wasn't one of those deaths by despair? I had every opportunity.

Dave Chapelle concludes that SNL monologue by imploring his audience, who probably overwhelmingly voted for Biden, to be humble winners, and he references those deaths by despair, especially among Whites likely to have supported Trump. "Everyone knows how that [despair] feels," he says. "But here's the difference between me and you. You guys hate each other for that. And I don't hate anybody. I just hate that feeling. That's what I fight through. That's what I suggest you fight through. You got to find a way to live your life. You got to find a way to forgive each other. You got to find a way to find joy in your existence in spite of that feeling. And if you can't do that -- come get these n i g g a lessons."

And I thought -- yes -- I know exactly what he's talking about. I've been getting those lessons all my life.

BORDER CROSSING

The rusty red minivan looked more pitiful than most. Officer Kofi checked the plates with his flashlight. West fucking Virginia? Good lord, they'd traveled a spell. Kofi didn't think he'd ever met anyone from there. He was surprised the place still existed.

Most of the folks waiting to cross that evening hailed from Upper Midwest, trying to sneak in before the first monster blizzard. So far, there'd been no snow, but the average temp had been flirting with zero for the past three weeks and it was barely September. Every year the cold came earlier and the storms grew worse.

There were four people in the minivan, all of their haz suits cheap and in questionable repair. A man was driving with a very pregnant woman sitting in the passenger seat. An older woman sat in back, most likely the man's mother, judging by their looks. A kid, maybe preschool age, was leaning against the old woman. Hard to tell whether it was a girl or boy. They looked terrified whoever they were. A family, Kofi thought, trying to escape from one toxic wasteland to a slightly better one, from one frying pan to another.

He motioned for the driver to put down his window. "Welcome to Crescent Region, sir," he said, making an extra effort to be pleasant since his supervisor had recently chided him for sounding like an android. "License, registration, and reason for travel, please."

The man reached into his inside door pocket and pulled the required papers. Kofi noticed his face shield was cracked and the pregnant woman's face shield was either fogged up or morphed to opaque. He couldn't be sure.

Kofi examined the man's license. His name was Abram Ruby; the minivan was an ancient turn of the century model with tags due to expire in a couple of weeks. Reason for travel: a letter from Flowers Energy stated Mr. Ruby and family were relocating to Crescent Region so he could work on one of their offshore platforms in the Gulf. He was due to report to work in two days.

"I see you're cutting it down to the wire, Mr. Ruby," Kofi said. "You're to report to the rig in two days. Mr. Flowers don't like folks to be tardy."

"I got here as soon as I could sir," said Mr. Ruby. He had a Southern accent thicker than Kofi's — as if such a thing were possible. His vowels were harder, though. "Traveling's not exactly easy these days."

"I assume you'll be headed to the company housing in 10 Zone East."

"Nope," said Mr. Ruby, smiling strangely. He pulled a folded piece of paper from his haz suit's breast pocket and gave it to Kofi. "I've got one of those golden tickets."

Kofi examined the letter. It was from the National Dome Lottery and stated, using a hundred words too many, that

Mr. Ruby's number had finally come up and he and his family were entitled to a two-bedroom unit in Dome District 10 South, the poorest section of the Dome. Most likely the unit would be smaller than a shoebox, but at least the family would have clean air to breathe and clean water to drink, an important perk with a baby on the way. Kofi looked for the official metallic hologram in the bottom right corner and scanned it with his handheld. Yep, the letter was legit and unexpired. Too bad Kofi was going to have to break this man's heart. "I'm sorry Mr. Ruby. This letter's no good."

"What?"

"Mr. Ruby," Kofi repeated, "this letter's no good now."

"That can't be. The reservation ain't expired. I double checked the date before we left."

Kofi took a deep breath. "According to the recent Supreme Court decision, Liberty City vs. the United States, regional rights trump any federal ruling pertaining to Dome residency." Okay. *Now* he sounded like a robot — but he figured that was the kindest way to deliver the bad news. *I'm just a drone. My hands are tied. Don't shoot the messenger.*

Mr. Ruby took a deep breath of his own. "Excuse me for cussing sir," he began, his reedy voice trembling, "but what the fuck's name are you trying to say?"

"I'm saying that here in Crescent Region your letter from the National Dome Lottery is null and void. Crescent Dome Board makes the rules, and what they say goes."

"Well ain't that a kick in the nuts. What am I supposed to do now? I've got a baby on the way. I can't live out in the muck! Why the hell do you think I left West Virginia?"

Mr. Ruby, Kofi wanted to say, *we've got hundreds of babies born in the muck here everyday. Don't see why you think you're special.* What he actually said was: "The only way into the Dome for you is to get a sponsor. Flowers Energy has a block of units in Dome District 10 South, but usually they're reserved for riggers who've been in region for a while."

That's when Kofi heard a voice, a small indignant voice, the voice of a child: *That's not fair!* The odd thing was he didn't hear this voice with his ears. It was pinging around inside his head like a thought, except the thought wasn't his own. He glanced at the child in the back seat. They had been cowering next to the old woman, but now they were sitting bolt upright, flashing him a stank eye for the ages.

"Excuse me," Kofi asked as gently as he could, "did you say something?"

You better not lay a hand on my son. Yet another voice pinging in his head. But Kofi recognized this one as Mr. Ruby's. What the hell was going on?

"I didn't say anything Mister," the boy replied with a slight, devilish grin. "I must've been thinking loud."

"Lillian!" scolded the old woman. "What did I tell you about messing with people like that?"

Lillian lowered his head. "That it isn't nice."

"Okay. So what do you do now?"

"Apologize," the boy whined. The old woman gave him a swift punch in the arm when he appeared to hesitate. "I'm sorry Officer Kofi for throwing my thoughts into your head. I should've asked permission first."

Then Mr. Ruby apologized. "I'm sorry too, Officer. I'm just very protective of my boy. I'm sure you understand."

Kofi didn't know what to think. It wasn't like he hadn't seen people with the gift before. His neighbor, Miss Willa, had the Sight, but to get her thoughts in your head she had to touch you first. Also, she said her gift didn't show itself until her late teens. This Lillian kid couldn't have been older than five and he could toss around thoughts like it was nothing; Kofi bet he'd be holy hell as a teen.

The driver in the car behind the minivan started honking and yelling. "Keep a lid on it, asshole!" Kofi yelled back. "We're moving as fast as we can." Meanwhile, Mr. Ruby and his clan needed a sponsor and a place to stay pronto or else they risked being booted from region. "I'll tell you what, Mr. Ruby. I'm going to put myself down as your sponsor. That and your letter from Flowers Energy ought to be enough to get you through."

Mr. Ruby hung his head. "Thank you," he said wearily. Then he added: "I guess."

"Listen sir, I'm really sorry about the letter. I really am. But the rules are the rules. I don't make them and I can't break them or it's my job and I've got a couple kids of my own. I'm sure you understand."

"Where are we supposed to live?" Mr. Ruby pleaded. He was desperate, on the edge of tears.

Oh fuck, Kofi thought, *please don't start bawling. My shift just started.* "I'll find you someplace. I promise. More than likely it won't be inside the Dome, but it won't be as far out as Tenth Zone either. That place is a pit. I'll give you your keycard and meet you in decon. Now exit to the right, please." He pointed the way.

At first Mr. Ruby wouldn't move and Kofi feared he might have a situation on his hands. But then the kid spoke up: "Daddy, I read him. He's fine. He'll take good care of us."

"Okay Lilly," Mr. Ruby said, somewhat relieved. "I'll trust you." He turned into the lane for the decon station.

Damn, thought Kofi as he watched the minivan pull away. That Lillian kid was something else. Miss Willa could also read people, but she had to be holding your hand at least. And you could feel when she did it too. It was a disturbing sensation, like ants tap dancing on your bare skin. But when the Ruby boy read him, Kofi felt nothing. He wondered if the whole Ruby clan was that strong.

Kofi radioed his supervisor: "Permission to leave my post, sir. I need to help a family through decon."

"Reason?"

"Special circumstances, sir. The woman's extremely pregnant. Plus, there's a young child."

"So? We've got Batista working decon center 3. She's good with women and children."

"No," Kofi insisted. "It needs to be me. I need to firm up some details with them."

"What details?" demanded the supervisor. "Nothing shady, I hope."

"No, nothing shady, sir. I just promised the kid special I'd meet them there."

"Okay. You got back up on your lane?"

"Yeah, Clark and Blackstone are here."

"Permission granted."

***

Kofi was glad to get away from the entry lanes, not that the border decon station was much better. He didn't care if Batista was on duty or not. Decon wasn't just about stepping in a chamber to zap all the contaminants from your gear; it was also about humiliation. During the medical examination they stripped, poked, and prodded you and asked all manner of invasive questions. It was like going through the old DMV except it was people, not cars. Mr. Ruby had just had his golden ticket shot full of lead; Kofi wasn't sure he'd pull through decon with his sanity intact.

And then there was that matter of Kofi promising the Ruby clan a place to live. Why the hell had he done that? Just because that freaky munchkin threw a thought in his head as casually as tossing a random piece of garbage? Or maybe: he'd just had it with making people needlessly suffer. He'd certainly want no child of his entering the world by way of the Tenth Zone. Might as well birth the kid in a garbage dump. And the Ruby clan had journeyed so damn far. *I mean, all the way from West Virginia in that hunk of tin.* They deserved better.

The red minivan was nowhere near the decon entrance when Kofi passed by, so he decided to take the long way around and make a phone call. "Hello? Father Avery?"

"Yes?" replied the tentative voice. "You've reached the Crescent Parish New Catholic Priory."

"Father Avery, it's me, Israel Kofi. Izzy? I volunteered at your homeless shelter back in high school?"

"Oh, Izzy!" the priest exclaimed. "How the hell are you? Haven't heard from you in a month of Sundays. You still working the border?"

"Yes, Father. That's kind of what I'm calling about. Do you have any room at the inn? I've got a family here whose golden ticket fell through."

"Dang." Kofi could just see the elderly priest shaking his head. "How long had they been waiting for their ship to come in?"

"Don't know. Didn't ask. But they came all the way from West Virginia. Looks like they might have sold everything they had to get here. There's a woman who looks like she's about to have a baby any day now."

"West Virginia? Didn't know folks still lived out there. I thought they'd fracked the whole thing to pieces ages ago. How many of 'em are there?"

"Four, soon to be five."

There was a long pause. Kofi prayed the answer wouldn't be no. Otherwise the Rubys would have to bunk at his place. That would be seven people crammed into his tiny cottage. His two teenage sons already fought enough. He couldn't imagine a preschooler and a newborn added to the mix.

"Um, let's see," the priest began, "homeless shelter's full. So's the halfway house. The only place I can offer is the storm shelter under the priory. The decor's late medieval dungeon, but we've got enough beds and clean linens and there's a kitchen down there. And: it's private."

"Thank you, Father!" Kofi was overjoyed. At least he'd have some good news to share. He was just about to congratulate himself for being such a wonderful person when he stopped in his tracks: "Father, there's something I ought to tell you about this family..."

Deep breath. "Oh? And what is that?"

"I think they all have the Sight. The boy especially."

Another deep breath — followed by an uncomfortably long pause. Father Avery belonged to the liberal wing of the church, and rumor had it he was even a member of the radical secret society, The Knights of the New Star. But generally, the nominally Christian religions had an uneasy relationship with those who had the gift. The more fundamentalist sects believed the Sight had something to do with the Devil and aggressively shunned those who had it. Catholicism didn't officially profess a problem with it, and most Catholics were fairly blasé, so long as you didn't flaunt your superpowers. Still, even some Catholics subscribed to the Devil theory. In the Crescent, the only traditions that took the Sight in stride were *Voudoun* and *Santería*. Kofi wasn't sure where his old mentor fell along that spectrum. Maybe one person with the Sight would be okay, but a whole family of people that could peer inside your soul? No thanks.

"How old is the kid?" The priest finally asked.

Kofi breathed a sigh of relief. At least Father hadn't said no outright. "Real young. I don't think he's five yet."

"Fascinating. They don't appear to be grifters, do they?"

"No sir, the father's got a job on a Flowers oil rig."

"And old man Flowers didn't sponsor him?"

"Apparently not. Probably because when the father got the job offer, the National Dome Lottery was still worth something."

"And Flowers is a cheap bastard — except when it comes to buying judges. I'll bet you my eye tooth Flowers was the baron who bought the justice who was the deciding vote in the case that gutted the Lottery."

Another pause. Kofi sent up a quick prayer. *Please Father, say yes.*

"I'll take them," the priest finally said. "Some folks here might have a problem with that, but what they don't know at first won't hurt 'em."

Kofi just laughed. "Thank you, Father. I owe you one."

"No skin off my teeth, Izzy. I do the work of the Lord."

***

By the time Kofi got off the phone with Father Avery and made his way back to the decon station, the Ruby clan had stripped down to their undies and were waiting for him in Decon Center 3. Officer Batista met Kofi at the door of Exam Room 1 and handed him the medical history questionnaire. "Well, Kofi, they're all yours. And remember: we're watching you."

"Just because I sponsored them in a pinch doesn't mean I'm going to cheat," Kofi said.

"I was implying no such thing," she huffed. Which, of course, meant she was. Batista might have been good with women and children crossing the border, but with her co-workers she had a rep as a back-stabber extraordinaire.

Kofi paused to collect himself, then opened the door. The first thing that struck him about the Rubys, now that they were standing up and out of full gear, was they were way taller than he imagined. (All except for Lillian, that is; he was small for his age.) Abram Ruby had to be at least six four; the grandmother (her name was Crystal Bannon Ruby according to the form) and the wife (Sabrina Charles Ruby) stood close to six feet. They weren't tall and broad, though. Abram Ruby was thin and wiry like a marathon runner; the expectant Sabrina resembled a beanpole that had swallowed a bowling ball and Crystal with her prominent nose and waist-length scraggly gray hair reminded Kofi of a fairytale witch. Most had coffee brown skin, but they didn't look Black, Mexican, Native American, or anything Kofi could put his finger on.

The boy was an odd mix of pretty and tough. He was so skinny he'd probably disappear if he turned sideways and significantly paler than the rest of his family. His wavy brown hair was unkempt and hung past his shoulders. He was going to have to get a haircut before he went to school or else he was gonna get his ass beat for looking too much like a girl. *And he'd have to change his name*, thought Kofi. *Who the fuck would name a boy Lillian?* Lillian wore antique style glasses with lenses at least a quarter inch thick, which meant when he was sitting in the family minivan with his glasses off and his haz suit helmet on, he was probably close to legally blind. His face displayed a kaleidoscope of fear, bristling attitude, and wide-eyed curiosity. Lillian looked like he could be a handful, but thankfully at the moment, he was well-behaved.

"Well, I have good news," Kofi announced. "Y'all got a place to stay. It's not in the Dome, but it ain't in Ten Zone either. A priest I knew back in high school, Father Avery, is going to put you up in the storm shelter under the priory in Six Zone. It ain't fancy, but there's a kitchen down there and it's private."

Abram and Lillian looked at each other and smiled. Lillian looked quite pleased with himself for reading Kofi correctly. "Thank you," Abram said.

Sabrina spoke next: "Are you sure he's gonna be okay with us living there? I mean..."

"I told him everything ma'am," Kofi said.

You told him about me? Lillian's plaintive voice pinged in his head again, although this time, Kofi didn't think he was doing it on purpose; the boy was just anxious, scared to death he'd ruined things for his family.

"Yes Lillian," he assured him, "I told him about you." He cleared his throat. "Now comes the unpleasant part..." He explained the medical history questionnaire. He'd interview them each separately, although Lillian, since he was a minor, could choose the one adult he'd like to accompany him. He warned them some of the questions could get pretty personal, but tell the truth anyway. "Cuz if you lie, it'll come back to bite you in the ass." He warned them the interview would be recorded. "This is to keep an eye on me as well as you." After the questions, came the doctor and the physical examination, one person at a time, except for Lillian who was allowed one adult present. "Oh and y'all can sit down. In fact, please do. You're making me nervous."

They sat in unison. Abram Ruby volunteered to go first, since A was first in the alphabet. Plus, he wanted to get the unpleasantness over as quickly as possible. "Can Lillian go in with me?"

"Sure," Kofi said, "if you don't mind him hearing your answers."

"Ain't nothing my boy don't know about me that he can't find out on his own."

Yeah I bet, Kofi thought. That was one of the disadvantages of having a kid who could literally read you like a book. Little white lies were out of the question.

Abram entered the interview booth first; Lillian followed. Kofi found it odd Abram didn't carry his son (because the boy was definitely small enough) or at least hold his hand — especially when he claimed to be so protective of him. They sat in separate chairs; Lillian had to climb into his. He struggled at first, but after Kofi gave him a quick boost, he was fine. That's when Kofi noticed the boy's eyes were different colors. The left was a strangely intense blue while the right was a golden brown.

Kofi began Abram's interview without introduction or fanfare. That's how you were supposed to do it, according to the handbook. Rapid fire questions, bang, bang, bang, your voice betraying little to no emotion. It was one of the few times when you were *supposed* to sound like a robot. The interview was as much about intimidation as it was about gathering information. *We know you're not worthy and these questions will prove it.*

Abram Ruby held his own. He was used to things like this. Most who lived outside the Domes usually were, even Kofi, who was in a position of relative authority. Every day you had to justify your right to exist and that job was never done.

Thankfully Abram Ruby was astonishingly healthy. Except for some bouts with asthma as a child, he was as healthy as a horse. Pretty impressive considering he hailed from one of the most toxic places on the continent.

Kofi turned his attention to Lillian. Kofi always found it strange that minors were required to have separate interviews. Why not just ask the parents? But sometimes kids hid things from their parents that might negatively impact their health — exploring dead buildings contaminated with industrial waste or worse, drug use, sexual activity — so it was better to ask. Although: the kids were also more likely to lie with an adult present. Kofi figured it was just more intimidation over information.

Before Kofi could open his mouth, Lillian had a request: "Sir, is it alright if my father leaves the room?" Surprisingly, Abram didn't seem the least bit surprised or flustered by this.

Kofi hesitated, although he wasn't sure why. Probably because the boy caught him off guard. "Lillian, that's really against the rules. I could get in trouble."

"Why? There's something I need to tell you and we need to be by ourselves."

Kofi glanced towards Abram, silently pleading for help. "But if we're alone, someone might say I tried to hurt you. That wouldn't be good for me and it might not be good for you."

"I know you won't hurt me. That's why I want to help you."

Kofi asked Abram: "Do you have any idea what he could be talking about?"

"He wants to repay you for your kindness to our family."

"I don't understand."

"Trust us," Abram said.

So, against his better judgment, Kofi let Abram leave and stand just outside the door. Kofi propped it open slightly, or else Abram wouldn't have been able to hear anything. *If Batista sees this tape, I'm dead.*

Kofi settled into his chair and was just about to ask Lillian the first question, when Lillian said: "Officer Kofi, you're sick. I could feel it when I read you in the car. And when you got me in the chair, I felt it then."

"I don't understand," Kofi said.

"May I put my thoughts in your head?"

"Why?"

And would you believe it? The freaky kid actually rolled his eyes at him. *So we can talk, silly.*

"Okay. I guess."

You don't have to talk either. I can hear you.

"Oh? So you're saying you can hear what I'm thinking? So what am I thinking now?"

Lillian recited a litany of his racing thoughts: *I hope this ends soon. This kid is freaking me out. I wonder why he has two different color eyes. Is that why he's almost blind?*

Damn. The freakozoid was right. *Someone should teach him how to play poker; he'd make a killing.*

Lillian giggled, clearly enjoying himself. But then he got serious: *There's a sore on your right arm near the inside of your elbow. You worry about it off and on. You were thinking about it when our car came up in line...*

Damn. Lillian was right about that, too. It had been there for nearly six months. It didn't get any bigger or worse, but it didn't go away either. Kofi knew he should get it checked, but he was afraid. Sores that hung around that long never signified anything good and what you didn't know for certain couldn't hurt you. Thing is: how could Lillian know that? Even Miss Willa couldn't read illness, even though Kofi had heard tales of people with the Sight who could. But this boy was only...

"I'm five," Lillian said out loud. "Five years, one month, three days."

Kofi quickly made a note of that on the questionnaire. Might as well look like he was doing something official. It might save his ass later.

I can make your sore go away, Lillian thought to him.

"How?" asked Kofi.

I can talk to it. Make the cells and the chemicals behave. It won't hurt.

"What do I have to do?" asked Kofi.

Unzip your sleeve.

Kofi was doubtful, but did as he was told. Lillian tumbled out of the chair, walked up to him, and placed both hands on Kofi's arm. Kofi could hear his heart pounding in his ears.

It's okay, Mr. Kofi. I won't hurt. Now breathe...

The boy closed his eyes, so Kofi followed suit. He immediately saw a flash of electric blue. The color was so intense, so visceral, it nearly knocked him breathless. Kofi'd never seen a blue so deep or vital. Then, he saw his arm as a camera might. He knew it was his arm, but he felt strangely detached from it, like it was a random object in a still life. Then, he saw a microscopic view: a dense and pulsing latticework of cells with each cell doing their part. The vision reminded him of the videos he watched in high school biology. And then: everything stopped cold, even time. He heard the boy exhale in slow-motion. It sounded like a mighty wave crashing back to sea. Afterwards the cells sprang back into motion, but now they moved differently, slow and deliberate, like they were being guided by an outside force. Damn. Was the boy literally moving his cells around like chess pieces?

Hush! thought Lillian. *You're really loud. Be patient. I'm almost done!*

Kofi tried to quiet his mind as best he could, but he'd never been one for all that meditation stuff. He wondered what the tape would show. A little boy holding his arm as he fidgeted?

There! Lillian thought triumphantly. *It's all better.*

Kofi was almost afraid to open his eyes. He didn't know which outcome he feared most. Had Lillian really healed him? Or had the last few minutes been an elaborate mindfuck designed to rattle him? He finally braved a peek. The sore was gone. "How?" he asked.

I don't know how, thought Lillian. *I just can.*

Kofi tried to zip up his sleeve, but couldn't because his hand was shaking too badly. After several attempts, he finally gave up. He thought about all the people on those religious shows who looked so unabashedly joyous after they were healed. Now he *knew* they were faking. Because a real life miracle was scary as shit.

Don't worry Mr. Kofi, Lillian thought. *I can help you with your sleeve.* The boy did the zipper as far as he could; Kofi finished the rest. *Please don't be scared. I promise I didn't hurt you.* He climbed onto a chair. His father returned and shut the door behind him. "You can ask me my questions now," Lillian said, grinning as if nothing had happened.

Oh yeah, the interview. Kofi had almost forgotten about it. "Thank you," he whispered. Then, he took a deep breath and continued with his job.

***

It was after midnight when the Rubys finally finished intake. Kofi called Father Avery when he got the word the last Ruby had cleared medical so the priest could meet the clan at the station and guide them back to the priory. Despite the fact the mist was high and visibility was close to zero, Father Avery arrived at the border in plenty of time.

Kofi was seated on a bench near the exit lanes keeping an eye out for the Rubymobile when the priest walked up and took a seat beside him.

"So Izzy," the priest began, "how are you doing?"

"Tired. It's been a long, weird day."

"I imagine days at the border are often long and weird, especially when it gets busy like this." He gave Kofi's shoulder a friendly squeeze. "Now Izzy: how are you really? You sounded a little — well — odd over the phone. You having doubts about sponsoring this family?"

"No Father," replied Kofi, "they deserve sanctuary."

"Then what is it?"

"I broke protocol during the interview and you know they record everything. I actually broke protocol escorting them through decon in the first place."

"So? You didn't do anything illegal, did you?"

"No, but if they watch the footage of that interview, I'm dead. The boy — his name is Lillian — was alone in the interview booth with me for a few minutes. There's always supposed to be an adult in the room with a minor."

"I see," the priest said. "And what was your reasoning behind your actions?"

"Lillian requested it. His father approved."

"Do you usually grant a five year old's request?"

Kofi didn't respond — at least not with words. Instead, he broke down in tears.

"Izzy? Are you okay?"

"Father, there's something else I have to tell you about that boy. Not only does he have the gift in spades; he's a healer. Who knows? Maybe they all are. And before you start telling me I'm bonkers, I know I'm telling the truth because he healed me."

"Really?"

"Yeah, I had this sore on my arm for ages. I know I should've gotten it checked, but I just didn't have time to be sick. I've got two boys to support. I just couldn't take the time..."

"First," the priest began, "I don't think you're bonkers. If the boy's got the Sight as strong as you say he does, it's quite possible he could be a healer as well. Second: fuck protocol."

Kofi laughed and Father Avery laughed with him.

"Seriously, I think you did the right thing. It is never wrong to be kind. That's a simple truth we often forget these days."

Kofi looked up to see the Rubys' red minivan exiting the center. He stood up and waved them over.

"You're telling me they drove all the way from West Virginia in *that?*" asked the priest.

"Uh-huh," Kofi replied.

"Huh. I guess there are such things as miracles."

***

That was the last time Kofi saw the Ruby clan in the flesh. After the family got settled in the shelter, Father Avery and the New Catholics filed the paperwork to officially become the family's sponsor. Kofi breathed a sigh of relief. He couldn't handle the family full-time; being responsible for his own two kids was more than enough.

Luckily, no one at the Border Patrol had time to review his interview tape. About a week after the Rubys came through, an Arctic snap gripped Upper Midwest bringing a snowpocalypse. Snow was seven feet deep in some places and the frigid temps rivaled those in Siberia. Those who could claw their way out descended upon the border in droves even though the Crescent's dreaded monsoon season had arrived with a vengeance. Snow or rain, take your pick. It sucked either way, but at least the rain was warmer.

Even though Kofi never saw the Rubys again in person, he did call the priory to check on them when he could. Abram Ruby made it to the oil rig in time; Sabrina had a healthy six-pound baby girl and named her Raylene; Crystal read a lot and helped Sabrina with the children. Lillian also read voraciously and spent his leisure hours helping the priests in the priory's indoor garden. "He has an incredible green thumb," reported Father Avery. "He talks to plants and they listen. Something else too: if it wasn't already obvious to you, the kid's a prodigy. We tested him for school and his IQ was off the charts. He'll probably be able to attend college at 9. And I'm sure every baron in the world will be chomping at the bit for a piece of him."

"So he's a genius *and* he's got the Sight?" said Kofi. "Double trouble."

"Well, he comes by it honestly. Despite that backwoods accent, the Rubys aren't hicks. Far from it. In a time long ago and far away, Abram, Sabrina, and Crystal were all senior government research scientists. Abram and Sabrina were geneticists; Crystal was a marine biologist."

"What happened?"

"No great mystery there. You know what happened: The Great Purge."

And because some clueless assholes decided they hated science, Abram Ruby was now working on an oil rig where he risked injury or death daily. What a waste. Kofi shook his head. Sometimes he wondered how Father managed not to lose faith after all these years — especially when God allowed stuff like that to happen.

"Oh: and Lillian wants to know if your arm's okay."

Since Kofi was safely indoors, he unzipped the sleeve of his haz suit to take a peek. The sore was still gone. Actually, he checked several times a day, just to make sure it all hadn't been a trick — although strangely, part of him hoped it was. Because truly: a miracle could be a frightening thing. Especially when it happened to you. "Tell the boy I'm fine."

"Will do."

"And Izzy?"

"What?"

"Trust me: your heart picked the right time to bleed. Every day I thank God you didn't turn those people away."

Approximately six months after the Rubys arrived in region, Father Avery called Kofi in a panic. Apparently the family had vacated the shelter without warning. Abram had left a note, effusively thanking the priests and Kofi for their kindness, but little else.

"Where'd they go?" asked Kofi.

"They claimed to have found a place, but damned if I know where it is. We'd been working to find them a permanent home, but so far, we'd found nothing."

"Any idea why they would have left so suddenly?"

"I think it might have had something to do with the boy. Some of the priests were uncomfortable."

Kofi glanced at his arm again. Seriously: was he going to keep checking for the rest of his life? "Well, he is extraordinary, and from what little I know of him, he's a nice kid, but all that power in such a small package? It's scary when you think about it."

The priest agreed. "Yep, Lillian and I had a heart to heart about that one night and you know what he said? *Sometimes, I scare me too.*"

STRANGE FRUIT

"She's stunning," said Tengo sullenly as Night made her entrance. "Now: why is she here again?"

"She's a damn good pilot," I replied, "and she's got a sweet shuttle that can fit us all. If we're gonna venture that far into the hinterlands, we're gonna need wings."

"She looks like another one of your, um, extracurricular activities," Tengo mumbled.

"Don't be an ass," I said. "She's also got the Sight like nobody's business and she's got as much of a right to be here as anybody."

Tengo rolled his eyes. "So you say…"

I rolled mine back. Screw him if he was jealous and wanted to pout. I grabbed Night's hand and introduced her to the rest of the crew: Sister Evita, Reginald Victory, Mother Amorette. Although they were superficially gracious, I could see they were all looking at her sideways too.

"Okay people," I said. "Out with it. What the hell is your problem?"

"She's whiter than snow," said Mother Amorette, who was the only one in the room who had ever seen snow since she was originally from Upper Midwest where it was omnipresent. "And she's a Domer."

"Not just any Domer," I countered. "This here is the one and only Nightflower, famed graffiti artist and activist who's been advocating for the Outside ever since I can remember."

"Art's one thing," said Evita. "Flying to a forbidden zone that's probably rated D6+ is another."

That's when Night decided she'd had enough of being talked about like she was invisible. She unzipped the right arm of her haz suit baring her forearm decorated with some of the sweetest ink I've ever seen. "Oh come on!" she shouted. "You all have the Sight! Why don't you fucking read me? Know my gifts! Know my heart!"

For a while all of them just sat there, stunned that such a luminously pale wisp of a woman could make such a loud noise. I just smiled to myself. I hadn't known Night for long, but I knew you didn't underestimate her. She wasn't your usual Do-good Domer dilettante with a guilty conscience; she was the real deal.

Surprisingly, it was Tengo who took up her offer to do a reading. He figured he might as well get to know the competition, although truthfully, Night and I hadn't done anything — yet.

***

Night was the one who approached me. I was hanging in the back room of Christy's at a table by myself people watching when I noticed this gorgeous pale woman clad in a skintight aqua blue high-end haz suit walking towards me. She stuck out like a sore thumb. You don't see many primo haz suits in the back room of Christy's. If anything, cheap haz suits with tons of patches are the order of the day.

That got my guard up. I figured she was some Domer girl slumming it, maybe some sorority pledge out on an initiation scavenger hunt. *Find some Deep Outside stud and screw his brains out. Post pics.* It was the season.

Instead she walked up to me, removed her gloves, and slapped her hands palms up on the table. *Read me,* she thought.

Huh, I thought back. *Impressive. You have the Sight. And you're strong enough to send and receive thoughts without touch.* I read her and determined she wasn't a threat.

"My name's Nightflower," she said as she sat down. Her voice was surprisingly deep, so much so, I briefly wondered if she might be a man — or even in-between. Either way it didn't matter, because like Tengo said, she was stunning. Her eyes were lavender. At first I wondered if she was wearing contacts, but then decided she wasn't. Although she was quite aware of her good looks and not afraid to use them, she didn't strike me as the type keen on artificial beauty aids. "May I buy you a drink?" she asked, then smiled. "A tall Blue Sky perhaps?"

I chuckled. "Really? A nice Domer girl like you came all the way to the Deep Outside for some booty?"

"No, I've been looking for you for a while," she said. "You're Papa Z or Zaden Storm, right? You turned down Lillian Ruby to his face."

I had been leaning back in my chair, but that got me bolt upright. As far as I knew, no one except me, Tengo, and my now estranged mother knew about me turning down a job offer from Ruby Biotech just before I graduated high school. The company had been eyeing me since I won first prize in the Crescent Regional Science and Engineering Fair back in junior high.

They offered me a sweet deal, I guess. They'd pay for my education anywhere in the world through graduate school. In turn, they would own my butt until my early 30s. I would have earned enough credits to live in the Dome and travel outside the Crescent and beyond. But when you're 18, someone owning your butt til your thirties is scary. Plus, I dreamed on it, and something about the deal didn't feel right, so I politely declined.

I'd had an interview with Ruby Biotech's number two, David Grove, and after he offered me the job, he gave me this business card with a private number on it so I could inform the company of my decision. I thought it was David Grove's private number, but no, the call went straight to the big man himself. And when I turned him down, Dr. Ruby just laughed and said he knew I wouldn't sign. He did tell me we'd work together one day though, so I didn't really feel bad about making what might have been the biggest mistake in my short life.

Mama, however, begged to differ. She threw me out of the house after graduation. Which is how I wound up living with Tengo. But how did Night know about all this?

Uncle Lilly told me, she thought to me.

"Uncle Lilly?!" I blurted aloud, and a few people turned to stare. *You mean you know the Boy Wonder of the Bayou personally?*

Yeah. I used to play in his house when I was little.

For some reason, I imagined her playing in the Ruby Biotech Tower inside the Dome, although Dr. Ruby never struck me as the type who would sleep in his office.

Apparently she caught a glimpse of what was in my mind's eye. *No silly,* she thought, giggling, *not there. I mean in his actual house. He does live in a real house, you know.*

"I know," I said aloud. *It's just that hero worship does strange things to your brain.*

Yeah, she agreed. *I mean I <u>know</u> him and sometimes I find it hard to believe he's a flesh and blood human being.*

What's he like?

He's cool. Probably cooler than you imagine.

Why have you been looking for me?

I hear you run a little salon to discuss matters beyond the veil.

I don't run it. I'm just a member. And I haven't been that for long.

Could you get me in?

Yeah, I could, but...

But what?

But why? You're obviously part of the Domer elite. Why do you want to crash some salon full of Deep Outside witches?

I hear you're exploring para-natural forms of protest, casting spells for the oppressed?

How do I know you're not some sexy Domer spy?

So you think I'm sexy, huh? She leaned across the table and blinked those big lavender eyes at me like she thought I'd be that easy.

I shrugged. *Yeah, I think you're hot. But so do you. Seriously: what gives?*

She straightened right up and threw back her shoulders. "I'm truly interested and, as you can imagine, there are not many people with whom I can discuss such things in the Dome." Now, there was fire in those lavender eyes. She was serious.

"Why would you want to protest your own kind?" I asked. "There aren't many who would sacrifice themselves, even for the good."

This system is wrong. And I owe a great debt to someone.

Suddenly I found it hard to breathe. That last sentence she sent weighed a ton. I mean, it felt like she'd thrown an anvil on my chest. I wondered: to whom did she owe that debt?

So will you put in a word for me? She was pleading now, like I was her priest and she was desperate for absolution. I thought if I said no, she might die right then and there. And no, it wasn't an act. She read true.

Okay, okay. So what skills do you have to offer? What's your superpower?

I'm a healer. And I've got a first class pilot's license and a couple of my own shuttles. I'm also an artist and activist. I started the Dome Youth Volunteer Corps when I was a teenager …

"Well, I'm not promising anything, cuz frankly, I'm not sure how the group will take to you. Sure you're aesthetically pleasing and you've got mad gifts. But you're also a Domer, you're white as a sheet, and you've got way too many credits to burn. That makes you hard to trust. We've been duped so many times before."

She lowered her eyes. "Fine," she said aloud. "I'll wait for your word."

Silence, but at least the air between us lightened a bit, signaling that uncomfortable business was over. "Do you still want to buy me a drink?" I asked, smiling.

She flashed those lavender eyes at me again. "Sure. What are you drinking?"

"Coffee," I replied. "I've got a long night ahead. A lot of code to write."

"Legal?"

"Technically. It pays well and I could use the credits since I ain't making those big Ruby Biotech bucks."

She laughed, then waved over a waitress and ordered something called Black Brazilian Thunder, which I'd seen on the menu, but never had the guts to order before. She ordered one for herself too.

"I will be able to sleep eventually, right?" I asked.

"Yeah sure. Frankly the name's scarier than the beverage."

Our coffee arrived: piping hot, strong, rich, and sweet. We talked some more, then left Christy's. She had her shuttle parked outside, so she drove me home. Since she had a tunnel pass, it took all of fifteen minutes. The ferry would've taken at least an hour.

Tengo wasn't home, so I invited her inside, but made it clear I had work to do and there'd be no hanky-panky. She was okay with that; she said she had her own work. She drew while I coded and it was nice having someone around, even if we weren't talking. Even though Tengo and I were partners, we spent a lot of time apart. Tengo ran a business and I scrounged for paying gigs all over. It made for some odd hours.

From then on Night and I ran into each other accidentally on purpose at various bars and clubs in the Ten Zones. We danced, talked politics, and once she took me flying just to prove to me she could do it. Every time we met, she asked about coming to the salon. She wasn't pesky about it; she'd usually just ask once and be done with it. I liked that about her: persistent, but not a pain in the ass.

I figured the best time to spring her on the group was when the group needed her special skills. We were headed on a ghost hunting expedition in the deep hinterlands, in the former state of Mississippi, someplace reachable only by shuttle. I hadn't seen her larger vessel, but I'd seen her navigate through the thick Crescent mist using only her sensors and her wits. Night was fearless. And that's what we needed.

***

Tengo held on to Night's arm for what felt like ages before finally pulling away and announcing she was legit. The room softened a tiny bit, but not much. Mother Amorette was still scowling and Night had to pass muster with her before she was truly in. Mother Amorette was the elder and had seen countless well-meaning Domer allies come and go.

"I think I've seen you on the ferry," she said. "Always sitting by yourself sketching us like we were figure models for your amusement."

Night opened her mouth to defend herself, but Tengo spoke up first. "She ain't drawing us for her art project. If she draws you, she means to heal you."

Night's jaw nearly dropped to the floor. She had no idea just how deep his reading had gone.

Reading people is Tengo's superpower, I thought to her. *You'd be well advised not to fuck with him.*

Noted, Night quickly thought back.

Meanwhile, Mother Amorette was circling Night like a vulture. Mother Amorette was a mountain of a woman, six feet tall and three feet wide. Night looked like a frail white hummingbird next to her. "Is this true?" asked Mother Amorette. "Can you heal people just by drawing them?"

"Sometimes," Night replied, "but not always. It depends on how deep the illness has gone. If it's gone too deep, I have to touch them."

"Touch them how? Are we talking laying on of hands?"

A wisp of a smile came to Night's face. "Well, I suppose laying on of hands would work, but I prefer sex. It's much more efficient and pleasurable for all parties involved."

Mother Amorette gave one last mighty scowl, then busted out laughing. "Hot damn! I like her!" she declared.

And that was good. All the tension in the room was starting to give me a headache.

Night visibly relaxed. "So: where do you need me to fly?"

"To the lost city of Natchez, Mississippi," Evita replied.

Night fiddled with her watch for a bit, then stretched out her arm to project a map of Crescent Region and the surrounding hinterlands onto the floor. "Show me where Natchez, Mississippi used to be," she said, and a red light started blinking about 200 miles northeast beyond the border of the Tenth Zone. She shook her head. "Man, that's deep," she sighed. "I don't think anyone's been that far into the hinterlands in a long, long time."

"Do you think you can get us there?" asked Reginald Victory. "And if you can't just say so. Don't be a hero."

"Show current weather," Night said, and the map transformed into a high-res 3D map complete with thick grayish green clouds of mist overhead. The quality of tech she owned was impressive. Tengo was even drooling and he sold the stuff for a living.

Night placed her free hand on her hip. "I've flown through some thick mist before, but..." She paused to point at a particularly thick patch of mist near our desired destination, so thick it appeared nearly solid. "...I've never flown through shit like that. Although I'm willing to try. Warning though: I'd be flying totally by sensor and it'll be a bumpy ride. Bring your own barf bags because even if you've never been air sick before, I guarantee you will be."

Stunned silence. Maybe Night was a little *too* honest.

"Why do you want to fly to the far reaches of the hinterlands anyway?" Night asked. "There treasure out there or something?"

"That's one of the legends about the place," said Mother Amorette, "but that's not what interests us. We're looking for a place called the Devil's Punchbowl."

"Well, the entirety of the Crescent hinterlands is Satan's Armpit," quipped Night.

That got a brief giggle from Reginald Victory. Mother Amorette shot him the stank eye to shut him up. "The Devil's Punchbowl was a post Civil War concentration camp for freed slaves," she explained. "Once the slaves were let loose from the plantations, many of them started to make their way up North hoping for a better life. A whole mess of them passed through the former Natchez, so many that the town's population swelled to over 100,000 overnight."

"Of course," she continued, "that was unacceptable, so the Union Army corralled them in these deep valleys by the Mississippi. They separated out the men and had them doing hard labor; women and children were left to starve and die. And die they did — men, women, and children — of starvation, of smallpox, of cholera, of hopelessness. They suffered so much, some of them tried to go back to the plantations, figuring this new hell was a hundredfold worse than the old one, but the Union fuckers wouldn't let them leave. And keep in mind, these are the folks we were taught were the good guys."

"Anyway," Mother Amorette concluded, "when the people died, they didn't get a proper burial. They just were buried where they dropped. Some say as many as twenty thousand died there. It's just one mass grave."

"Crap!" Night exclaimed. "I mean, I'm all about extreme travel, but why do you want to go there? The place is probably haunted as hell. A whole lot of violent death near water. An army of hungry ghosts."

"Honey," said Mother Amorette, "that's precisely why I want to go. Rumor has it that wild peaches grow there, but no one will eat them because they're cursed. I want some of those peaches; I want some of the seeds. I want to let these hungry ghosts finally have their vengeance — on the Dome."

"Does anything actually grow in the hinterlands?" Night asked.

"Truthfully," I replied, "we really don't know. As far as I know, no human has been where we're going in at least 50 years. But in my experience, once humans leave, Nature takes over fairly quickly. Even abandoned sites like Chernobyl are surprisingly lush — but they are still toxic. And haunted."

"How's everyone for haz suits?" Night asked the room. "They need to be top of the line and in good repair. If anyone's lacking, I'm willing to donate."

"Gees, Ms. Night," said Tengo, "you must really want in."

"I do," she confirmed. "And what the hell are credits for if you can't spend them?"

"So you will fly us?" asked Mother Amorette.

"Yes. Now, may I ask one question?"

"Shoot, firefly."

"How are you going to curse the whole Dome?"

"Frankly, I'm not sure of the spell," confessed Mother Amorette. "In fact, I'm not sure if what I have in mind is possible. I may be grasping at straws. It depends on what energy I find at the site and whether it's useful. I mean, that whole Devil's Punchbowl thing might turn out to be a myth." She eyed the thick mist on Night's 3D map. "We may not even get to our destination."

"I mean, why curse and not protest?"

Mother Amorette threw her head back and laughed like Night had told the best joke she'd ever heard. "Since when has protesting done any good? I mean, it may do a little good for a little while, baby steps here and there — better decon stations, a few more ferry stops, maybe a few well-placed donations by a few bleeding heart barons — but those are just band-aids. I want deep change, soul churning stuff. For that you've got to go beyond politics and policy. You have to do the impossible, go beyond the veil, confer with the ancestors, invite the ancient ones in."

"We Deep Outsiders aren't crazy or superstitious," she continued. "Certainly there are Domers born with the Sight who can perceive beyond the obvious. Those are the hearts I'm trying to reach."

"With a curse?" asked Night.

"You can't raise consciousness without a dark night of the soul. Domers will never understand the Outside unless they suffer like we do, unless they are made to live everyday constantly aware of Death's icy stare. Tell me, Ms. Night: who was the last of your Domer friends to die of an environmental cancer?"

"No one."

"Well, then," said Mother Amorette. And that was that. She was done explaining herself. Frankly I was surprised she deigned to explain herself at all.

Night said she'd keep an eye on the weather reports and report back with possible launch dates. There was some more chit-chat and after that the meeting started to break up. Sister Evita left for work at the hospital. Mother Amorette had to babysit her grandkids. Reginald Victory had errands to run. Which left me, Tengo, and Night awkwardly staring at each other.

"Is this a date night for you two or can I hang?" asked Night.

"Date night," Tengo blurted, and I just glared at him. I knew he was jealous, but he didn't have to be rude.

I was about to apologize, when Night held up her hands in mock surrender. "Listen man, I don't want to start nothing. I'll just leave. Catch you later, Z."

***

Since we weren't far from the house, and the mist wasn't too thick, Tengo and I decided to walk home.

"What the hell was that about?" I asked Tengo. "So what if I'm attracted to her. I got enough sense not to fuck her in front of you."

"It ain't that, Z," Tengo said.

"Then what the hell is it?"

"When I read her, I saw some things..." His voice trailed off and I started getting pissed. I hate it when he went all mysterious on me.

"What things?" I prodded. "Is she a Domer spy?"

"Hell no. Far from it. She wants change, radical change. She thirsts for it. But you know how I'm always saying there are two reasons for wanting revolution?"

Yeah, yeah, yeah. He expounded on that theory often. Some people want change because they sincerely want better lives for everyone; others want change because they seek revenge against a world they feel has wronged them. Most activists have a mix of the two motives, but hopefully the more positive one wins out. Because revolution fueled by vengeance only brings its opposite — devolution — in the end.

"You think she's primarily out for vengeance?" I asked.

"She has a real deep seated anger," Tengo replied.

"More than Amorette?"

"Yeah, if you can believe *that*. Oh: and about that gift…"

"Her ability to heal people by drawing them?"

"It cuts both ways. She can also make you ill. She can even kill you."

"Has she killed anyone?"

"Yes. I couldn't catch who it was, because that's when she cut me off. But it was when she was young and just growing into her power."

"She cut you off?" Seriously, that surprised me. Night had seemed so desperate to prove herself, I thought she'd made herself an open book. *Know my gifts! Know my heart!*

"Yeah, she definitely knows how to defend herself against a psychic attack," Tengo said. "Someone taught her well. Someone way more powerful than you or me."

"So if she knows someone that powerful," I asked, "what's her interest in me?"

Tengo rolled his eyes. "Other than the obvious?"

"No seriously: she sought me out. And she knows about my brief history with Ruby Biotech."

Tengo just laughed. "Well, I'm certain she's not the only Domer who knows about that. Not many people say no to Lillian Ruby. I'm sure he told more folks about that phone call than you think."

Now I was just getting annoyed. "Tengo, dammit!" I snapped. "Is there something you're not telling me?"

"Okay. She came to you because she'd heard about the salon. But mostly she's attracted to your power. She's looking for a partner in crime and thinks you're a good match. And: she thinks she owes you something..."

Damn. No wonder why that thought hit me like a ton of bricks. "Owes me *what*?"

"I don't know," Tengo replied. "Like I said, she threw up one hell of a firewall." Then he abruptly stopped walking and squeezed my shoulder. "Look man," he said solemnly, "do what you want. I don't really give a rat's ass whether you sleep with her or not. We've both done our share of playing around and we haven't lost track of where home is. But please, *please* be careful. I'm just looking out for you like you've always done for me."

It was true. I had looked out for him. Ever since junior high, back when he was a beautiful chubby boy who wore flawless makeup I'd been his protector and since high school we'd been a couple. Through thick and thin I'd been his North Star. Now he was strong enough to return the favor. "I'll be careful," I promised.

***

The Great Devil's Punchbowl Haunted Peach Expedition didn't take off until nearly a month and a half later. Night kept checking for a break in the weather, but the hinterland mist remained thick enough to chew until almost late July. Of course by then it was hot as blazes with daytime temps hovering around 110 degrees. No matter when we traveled it was going to be a shitshow. Mother Amorette finally called it: now or never.

We allowed a full week for the trip. Though our destination was only about 200 miles away, we had no idea where we were going since no one had been there in 50 years. We knew the Mississippi River flowed near, but it was toxic. We knew there used to be deep ravines in the area and maybe some poisonous snakes. But we didn't know if any human built structures were still standing. We might as well have been venturing to another planet.

Which made sense because we were dressed like mid 20th century astronauts. Night hooked us up with some industrial strength haz suits that were better than the gear Dome Public Safety wore, maybe even better than the stuff Ruby Biotech people wore when they ventured into a hot zone. Of course this meant they were bulky as hell and far from discreet. Even though our meeting place was far from the madding crowd in the dead of night, the few people who saw us eyed us suspiciously. They probably wondered what new environmental disaster Dome Public Safety was trying to cover up now.

It was a good thing Night sprung for those suits. Because we had to trudge almost two miles through the Tenth Zone to get to where she'd parked her shuttle. Now officially no one lived in the Tenth Zone because it was too toxic, but officially and actually are two different things. People did live there, just not anyone you'd want to know. Fortunately, everyone in our party knew their way around a laser pistol.

When I finally saw Night's ride, I was floored. Being a poor boy from the Upper Ninth, I hadn't seen many commercial class shuttles in my lifetime, but I'm sure her shuttle was ten times better. Jesus, this woman was loaded. Industrial grade haz suits for a party of six and now this?

"Holy crap!" exclaimed Reginald Victory. "This is *yours*?"

"Yeah," Night replied, shrugging her shoulders like it was no big deal, like everybody in the world had their own commercial class shuttle lying around.

After we finished gawking like a bunch of star struck idiots, we climbed in. The shuttle might have been spacious if we'd been dressed for a normal trip, but between our bulky suits and gear, it was fairly cramped. Night reviewed our route, then told us to strap ourselves in good, because it was going to be a bumpy ride. Mother Amorette insisted upon a pre-flight prayer and when we all joined hands, I felt everyone's heart beat through my fingers. Though everyone was playing cool, it was plain to feel we are all scared shitless. *Sister Erzulie*, I prayed, *bless my journey.*

Night wasn't fibbing about airsickness. Almost as soon as we left the Crescent proper, most of us were hunched over our respective receptacles. I've never ridden a roller coaster except in VR, but I'm sure that flight had to be ten times worse. Even Night had to set the shuttle on autopilot a couple of times so she could take care of business and she had done this before.

And the sad thing was we were just inching along. Part of the reason was because we were flying rogue; part of it was because the mist was some of the worst I've ever seen. And I suspect part of it was because Night was taking her sweet time because she didn't know what we would find once we reached our destination. Hell, I wasn't sure there was a destination to get to.

Eventually I felt well enough to go sit beside her at the controls. Tengo was too sick to give me the stank eye. There was nothing to see out of the window except thick churning clouds of mist. It reminded me of some of the photos of Jupiter I'd seen back in elementary school. Psychedelic hurricanes bigger than Earth.

So, I thought to her, *do you think we're gonna make it in one piece?*

She turned and smiled. *Sure Z.*

Her confidence was both reassuring and terrifying. *If we find this Devil's Punchbowl, what do you plan to do there?*

Just then the shuttle lurched sharply towards the right. Night's fingers flew across the screen and the ship righted itself. *I'll probably just read the place like Amorette.*

You planning on casting a spell of your own?

She smiled again. This time she was flirting with me. *You could say that. I'm just doing research.*

Research, I echoed, frowning. *Does this have anything to do with that debt you owe?*

She froze — and I thought I actually heard a door slam in her mind.

You mentioned some kind of debt in Christy's when we first met.

"I don't want to talk about that," she said aloud. I was making her nervous.

You know, I could crack that devious mind of yours open like a walnut and find out for myself, I thought.

"Not if you know what's good for you," she said.

I grabbed her arm. *Is that a threat, Missy?*

Why don't you try it and find out?

I let her go. Yeah, I probably could have cracked her mind open, but that would've pissed her off royally and she was my ride. I could fake my way around a shuttle, but I didn't have a license and I'd never fooled with anything close to hers. Plus, getting me and my friends stranded in the middle of the hinterlands wouldn't be a smart move. *I don't know what you're hiding — yet — but it better not be something that puts my friends in danger.*

She snorted. I could hear her cackling like a cheap horror movie witch inside her head. *You're already in danger. You're flying to a fucking forbidden zone.*

I mean more danger than we signed up for.

She turned from me and pretended to be completely absorbed in the patterns in the churning mist outside. I figured the sun must've been rising because the colors were becoming more vibrant. *What I'm planning has nothing to do with you,* she thought.

Fat fucking chance.

We hardly spoke for the rest of the trip, though I did hang close because I found staring at the mist strangely comforting, like getting toked up and staring at an old style screen saver like I used to do in junior high. Eventually I slumped over in my chair and fell asleep.

***

I awoke with a start nearly five hours later while the shuttle was in a steep descent. Night was hunched over the controls, watching her meters like her life depended on it, which it did. I scanned the rest of the ship. Everyone was still hunched over their receptacles, except for Tengo, but he wasn't looking too good. And I could feel the contents of my stomach slowly making its way up my throat. *So,* I thought to Night, *are we there yet?*

Believe it or not, she actually laughed at my weak ass joke. *Yeah, we're right above it. I'm trying to find a good place to land.*

Anything I could do to help?

Yeah, keep an eye on the controls while I go take care of business.

We both knew what that meant. So far Night had been the least sick of us all, but I suspected she'd been holding a lot in. We traded seats, which was harder than it sounds because at that point the shuttle was leaning sideways, and moving was treacherous. *What should I watch for?*

She pointed towards one meter flashing rapidly decreasing numbers in neon green. *Keep a watch on that. As soon as it gets in the red, push this button. The tech will do the rest.*

Why wait until it goes in the red? I asked.

Trust me, she thought.

I had a million other questions I could have asked, but Night was starting to look greener than a piece of moldy cheese. So I kept an eye on the numbers while she threw up bile. The numbers went red in less than a minute. I pushed the button and the shuttle seemed to hold its breath for a second before pitching sharply in the other direction.

"Jesus Fucking Christ!" swore Reginald Victory.

I looked at the screen. The mist was clearing and I could make out something that looked like dry land. We were landing. We had made it.

Night looked up for her receptacle. She looked as relieved as I felt as the craft gently touched down. "You're a good copilot," she said wearily. It was strange to hear her speaking voice after trading thoughts back and forth.

"Thanks?" I said. "I didn't do much."

"You did enough," she said.

It took a beat for everyone to realize we had finally arrived. It hadn't been the smoothest flight and I certainly felt the ghost of motion long after the shuttle had landed. While the rest of us stretched and tidied ourselves up a bit, Night checked the environmental conditions outside on her monitors. From what I could see through the screen, we'd landed in a lush tropical paradise. Green everywhere, mostly a mutant variety of kudzu, with giant leaves shaped like jagged stars. But looks could be deceiving.

Mother Amorette might have been one of the sickest while we were in flight, but once we were on terra firma, she was the first to recover and start asking questions: "So Ms. Night: what's it like out there?"

"Outside temp: 110 degrees, primary contaminants: ozone, petroleum byproducts, lead, low to medium level radiation," Night reported.

"Radiation?" said Tengo, surprised. "I don't recall there being anything nuclear around here."

"Doesn't matter," Amorette said. "You know the amount of illegal dumping is directly proportional to an area's toxicity rating. You don't know half the stuff that's in the Tenth Zone."

"Truth," I agreed, and everyone on board nodded their ascent.

"So Sister Amorette," asked Evita, "how long do you plan to stay?"

"Depends," Mother Amorette replied. She turned to Night. "How long do you think it's safe?"

"It's far from safe," replied Night. "Like I've said, I've done some extreme travel and this junket takes the cake. But I'll tell you what I've got as far as supplies: two emergency shelters that can hold two people a piece. They're the highest quality available and they should last you about two days. They'll take less than an hour to set up. The ground, at least in this immediate area, reads solid enough to hold us. I've got food for two weeks."

"But if the tents will only hold two people, where's the other two going to stay?" asked Reginald Victory.

"I'm staying with my shuttle. And someone..." Night glanced in my direction. "...can stay with me."

"How far are we from the former Natchez?" asked Mother Amorette.

"According to the censors, we're smack dab on top of it," Night replied.

Amorette closed her eyes and sent up a quick prayer. "Okay," she announced after a pregnant silence. "Gear up. We go out in twenty. First, we set up shelter; then we go exploring. We have 24 hours. No need of staying to the limit.

We either find what we want or not." She then assigned us our lodging arrangements. Evita and Reginald Victory in one shelter, she and Tengo in another, and me and Night on the shuttle, which is exactly how I would have called it, but since Amorette did it for me, Tengo didn't pout.

We hit the great outdoors in less than twenty, because truthfully, we had never fully geared down. And as soon as we disembarked, I realized why even the best haz suit I owned (and I owned some decent ones) wouldn't have cut it in the Deep Hinterlands. Not only was it hot as blazes, the air, even with my suit's filter running at full blast, seemed completely bereft of oxygen. By the time we'd set up the shelters, I felt like I'd run a couple of marathons. Tengo looked like he was about to faint.

Still, despite the place being hell on earth, it was oddly beautiful. Green, green, everywhere, with liberal pops of fluorescent color. Cicadas furiously buzzing in the background. I even heard the sound of rushing water, which I assumed was the mighty Mississippi. Seems the only time I heard rushing water in the Crescent was during monsoon season when water flooded the streets. Otherwise it just sat there and festered.

But even though the place looked like a new Eden on the surface, things seemed off when you got up close. Like the mutant kudzu I mentioned? I wasn't kidding. It really was *mutant* kudzu. And the vibrant flowers I saw? None of them were right. The petals were distorted or they were missing pieces. Not to mention that ant /praying mantis thing that crawled over my boot. And though I heard a cacophony of cicadas, I heard no birds.

We set up a meeting time and split up two by two by two. Our suits were all connected to Night's private network just in case any of us got into trouble. I stuck close to Night, even though I really wanted to be with Mother Amorette when she started reading the place in earnest.

Something about Night was unsettling me. I'm sure as an elite Domer, she was used to buying herself into places. But when I calculated the cost of her shuttle, our suits, the emergency shelters and our food, it seemed too rich a bribe for what we had to offer, even for someone who had so many credits everything was basically free. What did this trip mean to her?

She knew I was acting as her babysitter and said as much. "So: you keeping an eye on me?"

"You could say that," I said.

"Amorette wants you to," she said.

"That too," I acknowledged. "She probably heard us talking on the way here."

Night stopped in her tracks for a moment. "But I was careful not to *say* anything."

"Oh my dear naive rich girl," I teased, "you're so used to hanging in the Dome where most are dead of spirit. On the Outside, if you have the Sight, you learn to keep your antennas up and listening, since it may mean the difference between life and death. Mother Amorette's head might have been in a bucket, but I assure you, she was aware."

Night didn't have anything to say to that, and me calling her "dear naive rich girl" pissed her off, so we walked about a half hour in complete silence. Which was fine with me because it gave me the opportunity to get a feel for the place. Which so far felt like nothing like I had expected. I had imagined a full spectrum haunting with stunning visuals and peach throwing poltergeists. Instead, the place felt suspiciously inert.

"You know," Night mused, "I haven't seen any small animals around. I mean, like a squirrel, a mouse, or...a snake."

"Yeah," I concurred, "I haven't seen anything other than insects around." Of course as soon as I said that, a two-headed black snake slithered out from the underbrush. I waited while it went its merry way. "How much radiation did you say was out here again?"

"It wasn't much, but someone definitely dumped some shit here."

"Yeah, because this whole place is like the gods tried to remake Eden from memory, but their neurons were out of whack."

That's when Night punched me in the arm. "Look Z!" She pointed at a concrete dome on top of a steep hill. It looked like a scale model of Crescent Dome, probably a worker's shelter left over from when they still thought the Deep Hinterlands could be saved. I didn't see how we were going to get to it as we would have to climb almost straight up and even if we did manage to reach it, I didn't relish trying to get back down. But I could tell by the mischievous glint in Night's lavender eyes that she wanted to try.

Oh crap, I thought.

I thought you were quite the athlete in high school, she teased.

Jesus Christ. How did she know that? In all of our accidental on purpose meetings the subject of high school athletics had never come up. Maybe Uncle Lilly told her. *I was a baller, not a rock climber.*

Touché. And she started climbing.

Fuck you, I thought, and followed her up.

Actually, getting up there wasn't as difficult as I thought it would be as it took us less than fifteen minutes. I guess my body was getting used to the lack of oxygen. The shelter looked like it could hold maybe three or four adults comfortably. There was an electronic lock on the front door, but no way for me to easily hack it since it was a biometric lock. Not that I was keen on hacking it anyway it because something in or around that shelter was giving me a serious case of the spooks.

That's when I remembered those fancy haz suits Night had gifted us with came with x-ray vision. There was no need for me to waste brainpower trying to hack an impossible lock. "X-ray view," I said. My visor obliged and the cause of my unease became instantly obvious. Inside the shelter was a pile of bones, human bones, way too many bones for three unlucky hazmat workers who got trapped inside a shelter.

"Night!" I called, but she had wandered out of earshot. Either that or she was deliberately ignoring me. *Screw you.* I slid to the ground, which probably wasn't the wisest thing to do in a D6+ zone, but I figured Night's world class decon would take care of it. Besides: I was suddenly beat.

"Show me my party's location," I said, and my visor showed six blinking dots clustered in a corner. We really weren't far from each other, even though it felt like we were. Night was approximately 20 feet away from me. Tengo and Amorette were about 100 feet away in a valley somewhere; Evita and Reginald were 100 feet away in the opposite direction. I was far from alone. So why did I feel as if I were dangling from the edge of the universe? I figured it must have something to do with all those bones I was leaning against.

I decided to read the shelter, even though Mother Amorette cautioned us against reading a totally unfamiliar object on our own. But I wasn't alone, I convinced myself. My friends were near.

I did study up on my Deep Hinterlands history before the trip. The area had become D6+ due to a string of industrial accidents. The most recent accident was a gas explosion about 55 years ago. A construction crew was laying some pipe, a random spark flew, and boom, a massive fireball erupted. 10 workers were instantly incinerated; several more were injured. There were investigations, lawsuits, and recriminations, but eventually the area was declared a total loss and abandoned.

Still: the Dome-like shelter seemed like it was built way more recently than a half a century ago. Someone had been here since. Why? What were they looking for?

I removed my right outer glove and placed my right hand on the shelter. Then I closed my eyes, opened myself, and waited. I prayed the bones would speak quickly since I figured I had at most a half hour before my right hand was toast.

The bones did not disappoint. Almost as soon as I asked them to reveal their secrets, my soul was flooded with images. Only the bones didn't tell me their story; they told the story of the person who'd put them there.

There was a expedition. I saw a spry older woman with a shaved head trekking through the toxic jungle with three younger hikers: two men, one woman. I recognized the older woman immediately. She was Marta Andersen, rogue anthropologist and environmental activist, a fixture on any elementary school history site that was worth its salt.

Andersen's deal was that she'd stop damaging development or get much needed environmental rehabilitation services by proving sites were historically significant. Like some company would want to build a pipeline under a vacant lot and Andersen would come in and say, no, you can't do that, because under this lot is an ancient native burial site. And the company would say that's bulltinkie and Andersen would say, hold my beer, I'll prove it. Then she'd come in with her band of graduate students and state of the art proprietary equipment (most of which she'd designed herself) and damn if she didn't dig up proof. Along the way, she'd make some stupendous finds. Fossils of previously unknown species, artifacts from the Bronze Age. Officially, no one knows how she did it, but I think she had the Sight.

So Andersen's crew had been here after the site had been abandoned, which was unusual. Had she visited the site before the pipeline started? Had this been one of those rare cases Andersen lost?

I saw a fire, not a disaster fire, but a ritual bonfire. Andersen and her party each brought a pile of bones to place around it. The scene was macabre for sure, but I also sensed their intentions, and they were beautiful. The group encircled the bones, held hands and began softly chanting, lulling all those restless souls to sleep.

So that's why the place didn't feel as haunted as I would have thought. Someone had come before us to try to appease as many of those hungry ghosts as possible, and to give at least some of those bones a proper burial. But why had Marta and her crew risked their lives visiting a toxic abandoned site? Even if they did manage to secure land rehab funding, there was no way the site could be saved. Had they come to put the souls to rest simply because it was the right thing to do?

Oh Marta, I thought, smiling, *you were so damn cool*. And then: Night shook me out of my trance.

"Hey Z," she said, "look-it what I found." She held out three misshapen wild peaches in her hand.

It took a beat for my consciousness to swim back to the surface. I found my outer glove and put it back on. "What do you plan to do with those?" I asked.

"Take them back to the shuttle with me," she sassily replied.

"Night, you can't eat those."

"If you can sit on the toxic ground and take your glove off, I can risk a nibble. What were you doing anyway?"

"Getting a read on this shelter. It's full of bones."

Night sucked in her breath. "Damn. That's harsh."

"Marta Andersen and her crew were here," I said.

"You mean that anthropologist who had a knack for finding artifacts in the oddest places?"

"The odd thing is they came here after the disaster to gather as many old bones as they could and give them a proper burial. They didn't come in the name of science at all. They must've known the land was a total loss."

Night dropped the mutant peaches into the long pocket in her suit's leg. Now her right leg looked like it was growing a tumor. "So why did they risk their health over some old bones?"

"Don't know. Maybe the accident kicked something loose besides physical poison. Maybe it tore a hole in the veil and something snuck through." Just then I heard a ding in my ear. It was time to start heading back to the shuttle. Night, of course, heard it too.

I stood up, brushed myself off, and walked back to look down the hill we had climbed. We'd both have to be careful if we didn't want to twist an ankle or worse. I scanned the area for tree branches that looked sturdy enough to serve as walking sticks. It wasn't all that easy because much of the forest was smothered in mutant kudzu, but I spotted two likely candidates not far away and shot them off with my laser pistol. They fell to the ground with a thud.

"You're an excellent shot," Night said, as I handed her a gnarled branch almost as tall as she was.

I shrugged. "I didn't have any time to waste. I had to make it work."

She patted her leg, checking for the peaches.

"I think you should leave those up here," I said.

"Why?" she asked, frowning. "It's what I came here for. I bet you Mother Amorette pocketed some too if she saw any."

"And I'll bet you she didn't," I shot back.

"Well, I'm not giving these up."

Another warning ding sounded. I didn't have time to argue. I began my descent. "Slow and steady," I said as much to myself as to her. "Better a few minutes late than injured."

***

Our group gathered in the shuttle, shared some unappetizing MREs, and then gave our impressions of the site. Mother Amorette went first. "I sense the legends I've heard about this place are true, even though the energy here is far quieter than I would have expected. But it's an uneasy quiet. Like someone covered the top of a simmering volcano with a worn blanket to keep it from erupting. Leviathan sleeps, but fitfully..."

She continued: "Sister Marta Andersen has been here. I strongly sense her spirit. She tried her best to quell the unease of many anxious ghosts. And she did a good job -- considering. But it's only temporary. Decades ago, when that pipeline blew, something happened that has never happened before. Our poison and the wrath of the ancestors became one."

"What do you mean?" asked Tengo. Actually, I'm fairly sure he knew *exactly* what she meant; he just wanted her to say it plain.

"When all those ex-slaves perished here, their pain was forever etched in the soil," Amorette explained. "That's why no one here would eat the peaches. And then we poured our poisons on top of that and somehow the two things combined to make something new. The process isn't complete, and bless Sister Andersen for attempting to slow its progress, but someday this beast will be born."

Everyone inhaled sharply -- everyone except Night. I actually thought I caught a wisp of a smile on her face, like she had been waiting for something like this to happen.

"I will not," Mother Amorette proclaimed, "disturb the darkness brewing here to cast a spell. My righteous anger seems petty now. Not even Domers deserve what may be coming."

And that's when it hit me. This place didn't exactly feel quiet; it felt like it was holding its breath, waiting for just the right moment to exhale. It felt like a cloud before a storm, bloated with rain.

That should have been the end of it. Mother Amorette had spoken and she said the spell was off. Didn't matter what anyone else thought, even though we all had an opportunity to speak on our impressions. Mother Amorette knew what she was talking about. She led us in one final prayer; then we split into our assigned shelters to sleep for a few hours before the flight home.

***

Night and I decontaminated ourselves and climbed into the shuttle. I kept thinking about those peaches she'd stashed in her pocket and I must've been thinking about them hard enough to disturb her because she kept swatting at the air in an attempt to swat my thoughts away.

"You heard Amorette, Night. Ditch the damn peaches."

No way, she thought to me. *I didn't fly through all that mist to go home empty-handed.*

We're not doing the spell. We don't know what kind of energy is growing here.

"You mean you guys aren't doing the fucking spell!" she snapped. "I found just what I wanted!"

"Goddamn it, Night! I got you into this salon!"

"And I took you on your little field trip, so I guess we're even!"

She retrieved the peaches from her pocket and set them on the control panel. Then she opened a hidden compartment under one of the pilot's chairs and pulled out a black satchel. From the satchel she pulled a small vial of dark indigo liquid, two pocket hypos, and a piece of rubber tubing.

I knew exactly what the liquid was: Blue Sky. But it was several orders of magnitude stronger than the peacock blue bar piss variety. She'd either scored it on the black market or paid a chemist to whip up a batch especially for her. Normally, the only reason someone with gifts of her caliber would use Blue Sky is if they were a psychic for hire and working on a deadline. But even they wouldn't mess with stuff that potent. And they *certainly* wouldn't mainline the shit. That would crack your soul wide open, shatter it into a million pieces, never to be heard from again.

What the fuck are you doing? I asked.

Research, she replied, as she tied the piece of rubber around her arm and poked around for a vein.

"Well, I'd wish you'd save your 'research' until after you fly us home," I said aloud.

She replied by tuning me out completely. She examined the three peaches on the console, chose the one that was shaped like a baboon butt, and cut off a small piece with a switchblade she carried in her suit. Then she briefly closed her eyes, whispered a quick prayer to fate, and popped the piece into her mouth. She chewed it slowly, making a face as she did. I wondered: what did a cursed and slightly radioactive peach taste like? Was it bitter? Was it tough? Or was it preternaturally sweet?

After she'd ingested the peach, she filled the pocket hypo and injected the Blue Sky. Since she was mainlining, the drug's effect was immediate. She leaned back in the chair and would have damn near flipped out of it if I hadn't caught her. I found myself on the floor, holding her limp body in my arms. Yeah, I did want to get up close and personal with her, but not like this.

I've never mainlined Blue Sky. In fact, I make it a policy never to do anything stronger than bar piss and I don't do that very often. My gift is too strong for that kind of foolishness. That's not a brag; it's just the truth. When you have the gift, the first thing you have to learn is how not to get overwhelmed by all the extra sensations. You learn not to hear everyone's stray thoughts when you ride the ferry, things like that. But Blue Sky puts the kibosh on your filters. Suddenly it's second puberty all over again and I wouldn't wish that on anyone.

Night's lavender eyes looked almost black because her pupils were as large as saucers. She was breathing, but barely. I synced my breath with hers and established a casual link, strong enough to sense trouble, but weak enough to break easily if my soul needed to make a run for it.

She wasn't seeing any visions yet. All I saw when I got behind her eyes was the shuttle's interior in blurry soft focus. I could hear something in the distance, though: men's voices chanting and the rhythmic clink of hammers. A ghostly chain gang? Or the freedmen the Union soldiers sentenced to hard labor?"

Then suddenly: Night's body stiffened and her breathing grew labored. Out of the corner of my eye, I could see a red light on my suit blinking, indicating a member of my party was in bodily trouble. All of our suits had one and right now they would all be blinking in unison. I prayed no one else would notice it and come to the shuttle to check things out. That's just what I didn't need. Amorette would've read me the riot act about Night and the peaches.

Fortunately no one came, but that didn't solve my immediate problem. Night was having a seizure and since I was linked to her, I was starting to have one, too. I willed my vital signs to slow; I imagined the fresh, metallic scent in the air after a thunderstorm; I saw myself as a bird taking refuge in the hurricane's eye — anything to quell the tempest brewing in us. *Night, I swear: if you die on me, I'm gonna raise you up so I can kill your ass again.*

The threat seemed to work. Night's body relaxed; her breathing became closer to normal, and my head stopped feeling like it had been repeatedly tased. Also, the light on my suit stopped blinking.

But we weren't out of the woods yet. The visions from the peach were just beginning. And it was the full-spectrum haunting I'd been dreading...

We lose ourselves in the body of a woman, so thirsty the inside of our mouths taste like rust, so hungry our stomach has begun to eat itself. On the ground before us lay an infant, bloody and deformed, stillborn. Our fingers so thin and brittle, they look like twigs. We pray to Jesus, to the Father, to the sweltering sun they created, to let us die now. We look to the sky. It is milky white, no wind in the trees...

JUMP CUT

We have landed in a different woman. Walking. There are many. Carrying everything we own upon our backs. A few horses, bony and sick, lope beside us.

JUMP CUT

Now we are lost in the body of a man who is hiking through the desert with his children. We hear water in the distance. Another man points ahead. Aquí, he says, but his accent is off, the harsh twang of a gringo. Do we trust him?... We remember a old children's rhyme:

Ophelia and her father sleeping underwater

Dreaming of a land of milk and honey

While fat white cats are counting money...

Hey! Wait a damn minute. I managed to wrest myself away from the horrific montage. Something was terribly wrong. All of this didn't come from one peach. The visions weren't even from the same geographical area or time. The first woman was a slave; the second was walking the Trail of Tears; the man was part of the great Central American migration at the turn of the century just when the shattered states were showing their first cracks. When my father's people came...

Holy crap! Night was a collector! She collected ghosts, digested them, and then stored them for later use. And who knows how long she'd been gathering energy from the darkest hauntings in history. That's when I realized: that firewall she'd erected wasn't to keep Tengo out; it was to corral all that stuff in. But why? Did she get off on pain? Was this some hackneyed way to atone for Domer sins?

Truth was, I didn't have time to ponder the philosophical implications of it all because Night was way past capacity. That final dose of Blue Sky had done it. All those restless ghosts were running amok and soon they would drown her out. Then she'd be stark raving mad and I'd have to try to get us home.

Time for drastic action. I needed to eat some history. *Night!* I thought to her. *Can you hear me?*

No answer. I took a brief dip behind her eyes and realized it was useless. The visions were parading by so fast and furious, it was like watching white noise. Soon her vitals were going wild and the warning light on our suits started blinking again.

I laid her on the floor. Her lavender eyes were a study in raw fear. Which was good. It meant there still was enough of her around to know to be afraid. "I don't know how long you've been carrying that shit around," I said, "but you're gonna have to let some go."

She groaned and made a sorry attempt to wiggle away. But she could barely move.

"No, honey," I said, frantically unzipping her out of her suit, "you can't carry it for much longer."

Yes...I...can, she thought. Then she went stiff as a board.

I tore off my suit, threw myself on top of her, then held on for dear life. We were skin to clammy skin, our hearts racing as one. I looked her dead in the eye. "Give it to me," I said.

She hesitated. She didn't want to give up any part of her collection.

"Give it to me, Night," I pleaded. "Or you'll die. I ain't playing." Maybe I was crying by then; I really can't remember. All I know is that I've never been so scared in my life.

She groaned again -- then went limp.

No, no, no you don't! I kissed her -- as a wave of ghosts crashed through me, more than I could swallow.

But at least it relieved enough pressure for her to move. And move she did, grabbing onto me for dear life. We had sex, but it was like fucking on a raging battlefield as the dead watched. No love in it at all, or even lust; there was only desperation, food for hungry ghosts.

***

We awoke in a puddle of our own sweat. Night was still groggy, hungover from Blue Sky and ghosts, so it fell on me to clean things up. I let her drift between sleeping and waking while I got washed and geared up. I didn't have much to say to her anyway.

 I went outside to the emergency shelters to check on the rest of the crew. Everyone was still asleep and snoring, dead to the world. Only then did I check the time. Just 6:00 AM. Hard to believe all that happened before the crack of dawn.

But it was good it was still early because I had one important piece of business: get rid of those damn peaches before Mother Amorette caught a whiff of them. Night was going to be pissed, but I didn't much care what she thought. She almost stranded us in the Deep Hinterlands; she didn't deserve a vote.

I didn't walk far. Just 200 feet from camp. I threw that mutant fruit in the direction of the sound of rushing water, chanting a banishing spell while I did. Then: I hoped it was over, though I still had to take care of myself. I'd swallowed a lot; my soul ached. But I figured I was strong enough to keep things in check until I got home.

That's when it hit me: suppose Night had staged this whole escapade as a test. Tengo had said she wanted a partner in crime, someone as strong as she was. And despite the night of ghosts, Night had revealed herself to be plenty strong, once in a generation strong in fact. If she hadn't tipped the scales with that Blue Sky, she would still be toting around that little shop of horrors with none of us being the wiser. Most people's souls would have cracked under the strain.

When I got back to the shuttle, Night had geared up and was in the midst of doing a pre-flight check. The satchel with the Blue Sky and paraphernalia was safely stashed in the secret compartment.

"You gonna be okay to fly?" I asked.

"Yes, I'm fine," she replied, eyes glued to the console.

"That was some stunt you pulled last night."

"Listen: I know you're mad at me, but I don't feel like fighting right now."

"Okay. I'm not fighting, but I do want to let you know that you scared the shit out of me. And you did the one thing I warned you not to do: you put my friends in danger."

Only then did she look at me. "Don't be so melodramatic, Z. You could've flown this shuttle home. You would've saved your friends. Hell, even though you were madder than a snake at me, you saved my life."

"You place too much faith in me," I said.

She rose from the console, walked up to me, lifted my helmet visor, and placed her hand on my cheek. It was still humming from the night before and I heard the ancestors whispering around us. I was still angry, and she scared me to my bones, but there was still something seductive about the dark magic we made together. Even though I knew I should have pushed her hand away, I didn't.

"I do not place too much faith in you," she said. "I haven't placed enough. I see why Uncle Lilly wanted you."

I didn't know what to say to that, so I just stupidly stared at her for who knows how long. "I don't think you should come to the salon anymore," is what I finally said.

"Fair enough," she agreed, her hand still resting on my cheek.

"Is this...I mean, was this...a test?"

"Nope," she replied. "But what happened happened for a reason."

That's when I pushed her hand away. At least I tried. But she caught me in some ninja tango move and suddenly our faces were inches apart. Ghost energy buzzed around us like a swarm of hungry mosquitoes. Yes, it was bone-chilling, but it was also electric. She kissed me, and for an instant, I was ready to give in to her sick fantasy: I thought we could rule the world.

***

The trip back wasn't half as sick–making, thank god. I hung back with Tengo where it was safe. Occasionally Night would steal a glance at me from the pilot's chair, but I'd grip Tengo's hand and close my eyes to avoid her gaze.

What the hell did she do to you, Z? Tengo thought to me.

I don't want to talk about it, I replied. And I shut my mind like a steel trap. He didn't try to read me. He knew better.

When we finally arrived in Crescent Region proper, Night parked the shuttle in the Tenth Zone and all us Deep

Outsiders started trekking to our respective homes. Only then did Mother Amorette pull me aside.

Oh crap, I thought, *she's gonna throw me out of the group.* Because I knew she sensed something big had gone down and it wasn't good and it was my fault.

But Amorette surprised me. She wasn't pissed; instead she was worried. "Are you okay?" she asked.

"I'm sorry," I said.

"Sorry for what?"

I didn't feel like telling her the whole story, a good part of which she probably knew anyway, so I just grabbed her hand and fed her images.

"I see," she said. "But I say you did the best you could. And you're right: she is strong. But you are stronger." Then: "Keep an eye on her for me, will you?"

"What?" I asked, flabbergasted. Because at that point I wasn't sure I ever wanted to see Night again. I mean, she was hot, but that night I spent with her was far from the most pleasurable I've had.

"You can handle her, so you watch what she does."

"Why?"

Amorette smiled. "Because I know you relish a challenge. And you just might have to save us again."

FINAL THOUGHT

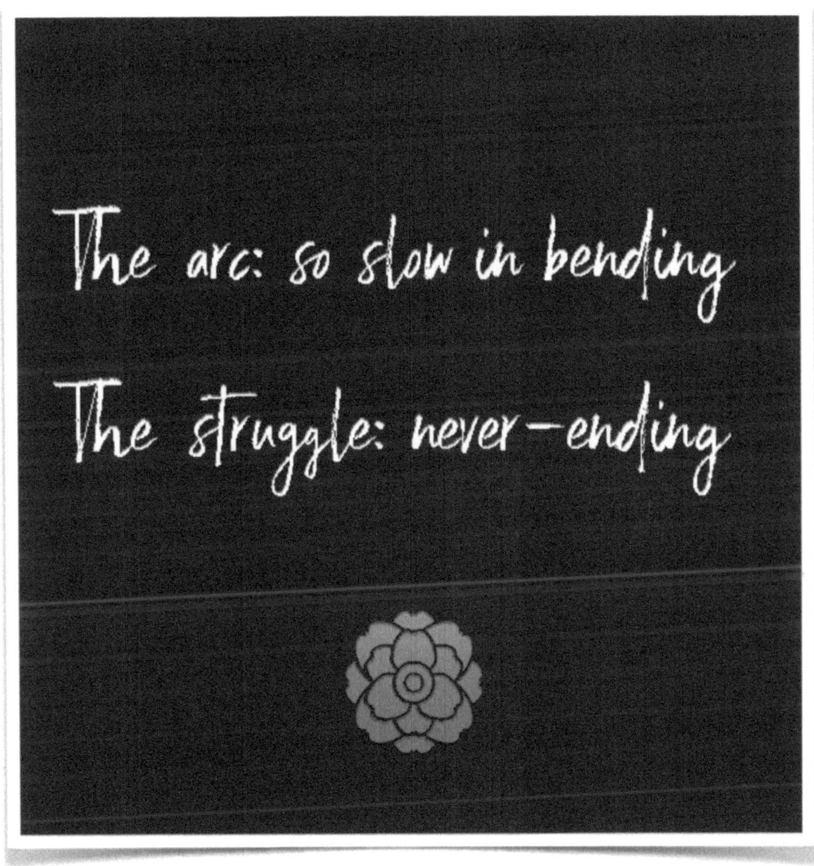